THE SECULAR SCRIPTURE
A Study of the Structure of Romance

The Charles Eliot Norton Lectures, 1974-1975

Northrop Frye

The Secular Scripture

A Study of the Structure of Romance

HARVARD UNIVERSITY PRESS
Cambridge, Massachusetts, and London, England

Copyright©1976 by the President and Fellows of Harvard College
Fifth printing, 1982

Library of Congress Cataloging in Publication Data

Frye, Northrop.
    The Secular Scripture.

    (The Charles Eliot Norton Lectures; 1974-1975)
    Includes index.
    1. Romances—History and criticism—Addresses, essays, lectures.
I. Title. II. Series.
PN56.R6F7   809′ .91′4   75-37627
ISBN 0-674-79675-6 (cloth)
ISBN 0-674-79676-4 (paper)

To my Harvard-Radcliffe students, 1974-1975

Preface

THERE IS NOT much to say about this book except that it contains the lectures which I gave as Charles Eliot Norton Professor of Poetry at Harvard University in April 1975. This came at the end of an exhilarating and most profitable year in residence at Harvard. To record the personal obligations of my wife and myself to the kindness and hospitality of my Harvard colleagues would swell this preface into a long, and for them embarrassing, catalogue. So I have simply dedicated the book to my students: the fact that there were several hundred of them indicates another aspect of Harvard's friendliness to a visitor.

Those familiar with my other work will find many echoes of it here, from the Schiller reference at the beginning to the Hippolyta one at the end. However, the book has its own place in my writing as a very brief and summary geography lesson in what I call the mythological or imaginative universe. Most of my scholarly interests at present revolve around the thesis that the structure of the Bible provided the outline of such a universe for European literature. The present book is based on that thesis, though concerned with secular literature, and there are many references in it, including its title, to this aspect of its argument.

A book based on public lectures can hardly be organized on a basis of documentation: there are practically no notes, and only two or three examples are given out of many hundreds of possible ones. Many readers will readily think of better examples; but if they are interested in the general idea, they may use this book as a kind of figured bass on which to develop their own progressions. Even if there is ultimately only one mythological universe, every reader sees it differently.

N.F.

Victoria College
Massey College
University of Toronto
July 1975

Contents

The Word
and World of Man

THIS BOOK IS concerned with some principles of storytelling. The discussion revolves around fiction, and especially around what I am going to call naive and sentimental romance, using two critical terms derived from Schiller's essay *On Naive and Sentimental Poetry.* I am not using these words precisely as Schiller uses them—I could not bring myself to call Goethe a naive poet, as he does—but they are not used in quite their ordinary English senses either. By naive romance I mean the kind of story that is found in collections of folk tales and *märchen,* like Grimms' Fairy Tales. By sentimental romance I mean a more extended and literary development of the formulas of naive romance. Most of this, in early and modern times, has been in prose narrative.

Sentimental romance begins, for my purposes, in the late Classical period. There is Greek romance in Heliodorus, Achilles Tatius, Longus, Xenophon of Ephesus, and others. There is Latin romance in Apuleius and (probably) the Apollonius story, used twice by Shakespeare. And there is early Christian romance in the Clementine Recognitions, in the story of Barlaam and Josaphat, and the more legendary lives of the saints. This literature covers a period of many centuries, and none of it except Apuleius'

Golden Ass is generally familiar, but I have to refer to it occasionally because it shows the stock themes and images of romance with special clarity, as early works in a genre so often do.

Medieval romance presents different structural problems, which I shall have to touch very lightly. But in sixteenth-century England, with Sidney's *Arcadia* and similar works, the late Classical conventions reappear. When the novel developed, romance continued along with it in the "Gothic" stories of "Monk" Lewis and his Victorian successors. William Morris is to me the most interesting figure in this tradition for many reasons, one of them being his encyclopedic approach to romance, his ambition to collect every major story in literature and retell or translate it. In the twentieth century romance got a new lease of fashion after the mid-fifties, with the success of Tolkien and the rise of what is generally called science fiction.

No genre stands alone, and in dealing with romance I have to allude to every other aspect of literature as well. Still, the conventions of prose romance show little change over the course of centuries, and conservatism of this kind is the mark of a stable genre. In the Greek romances we find stories of mysterious birth, oracular prophecies about the future contortions of the plot, foster parents, adventures which involve capture by pirates, narrow escapes from death, recognition of the true identity of the hero and his eventual marriage with the heroine. We open, let us say, *Guy Mannering*, written fifteen centuries later, and we find that, although there are slight changes in the setting, the kind of story being told, a story of mysterious birth, oracular prophecies, capture by pirates, and the like, is very much the same. In Greek romance the characters are Levantine, the setting is the Mediterranean world, and the normal means of transportation is by shipwreck.

In science fiction the characters may be earthlings, the setting the intergalactic spaces, and what gets wrecked in hostile territory a spaceship, but the tactics of the storyteller generally conform to much the same outlines.

One of the roots from which these chapters grew was an abandoned essay on the Waverley novels of Scott. The home I was brought up in possessed a good edition of the Waverley novels, and I had, I think, read them all in early life, with utter fascination. Some years later, at college, *Guy Mannering* was on a course and I reread it, but I had entered the age of intolerance by then, and *Guy Mannering* now seemed to me only a clumsy and faked narrative with wooden characters and an abominable style. I read Scott as little as possible through my earlier professional life, but about twenty years ago I was talking to a late friend whose name it is a pleasure to mention here, Richard Blackmur, about the amount of tedium in modern life caused by plane journeys and waiting in airports. He remarked that he had got through a long and exhausting trip himself with the aid of Scott. "I love Scott," he said. I tried the recipe. Richard was right, as he so often was: when one is traveling by jet plane it is deeply reassuring to have a stagecoach style for a traveling companion.

By this time I was ready to become fascinated once more by Scott's formulaic techniques. The same building blocks appeared every time: light and dark heroines, outlawed or secret societies, wild women chanting prophecies, heroes of mysterious and ultimately fortunate birth; but the variety with which they were disposed was what now impressed me. I noticed that much of the criticism of Scott attempted to assimilate him to standards that were not his. It was said that his characterization was what was important and that his plots were of secondary interest: this is nonsense, of course, but was said about him because it is believed to be true of more fashionable writers. After I began to glimpse something of the uniformity of romance formulas over the centuries, I understood that my interest in Scott belonged in a larger context.

Meanwhile, an early absorption in Blake had expanded in two directions. One direction took me into the Bible by way of Milton: this is to be explored in another book. The other direction was one that connected Blake with two other writers in particular, Spenser and William Morris, both writers of sentimental romance. So Spenser, Scott, and Morris appeared as three major centers of romance in a continuous tradition, and, these once identified, other centers, like the tales of Chaucer and the late comedies of Shakespeare, soon fell into place. This left me with a sense of a double tradition, one biblical and the other romantic, growing out of an interest in Blake which seemed to have contained them both. The title of this book, *The Secular Scripture*, suggests something of its relation to a study of the Bible. The distinction underlying this relation is our first step.

Every human society, we may assume, has some form of verbal culture, in which fictions, or stories, have a prominent place. Some of these stories may seem more important than others: they illustrate what primarily concerns their society. They help to explain certain features in that society's religion, laws, social structure, environment, history, or cosmology. Other stories seem to be less important, and of some at least of these stories we say that they are told to entertain or amuse. This means that they are told to meet the imaginative needs of the community, so far as structures in words can meet those needs. The more important stories are also imaginative, but incidentally so: they are intended to convey something more like special knowledge, something of what in religion is called revelation. Hence they are not thought of as imaginative or even of human origin, for a long time.

The more important group of stories in the middle of a society's verbal culture I shall call myths, using that word in a rather specific way which would not apply without modification outside the present argument. The more peripheral group, regarded by its own society, if not necessarily by us, as less important, I shall connect chiefly with the word folktale, though other words, such as legend, also belong to it. It is difficult to make an adjective out of the word folktale, so I shall speak of my two types of verbal experience as the mythical and the fabulous.

In European literature, down to the last couple of centuries, the myths of the Bible have formed a special category, as a body of stories with a distinctive authority. Poets who attach themselves to this central mythical area, like Dante or Milton, have been thought of as possessing a special kind of seriousness conferred on them by their subject matter. Such poems were recognized, in their own day, to be what we should now call imaginative productions; but their content was assumed to be real, if at one remove, and not only real but about what most deeply concerned their readers.

When we turn to the tales of Chaucer or the comedies of Shakespeare, the primary motive of the author seems to be entertainment, in the sense of the word just used. Here we notice an influence from folktale, so pervasive as to make it clear that folktale is their direct literary ancestor. There are hardly any comedies of Shakespeare, and few tales told on the Canterbury pilgrimage, that do not have some common folktale theme prominently featured in them. In Greek literature, the central mythical area is provided mainly by the Homeric epics and the tragic poets. The comic writers are allowed to be more inventive, and tell stories that have no connection with the Greek equivalent of revelation, though, as in *The Birds* and *The Frogs*, they often parody it. Again we notice, as we go from New Comedy to the later prose romances, an increasingly close connection with folktale.

Most myths are stories about or concerning the gods, and so the distinction between the mythical and the fabulous overlaps a good deal with the distinction between the sacred and the secular. But it is not identical with it, since many stories may be mythical, in the present sense, without being sacred. The largest and most important group of these are the national stories, which as a rule shade insensibly from the legendary to the historical. "In addition to the Bible," says George MacDonald, "each nation possesses *a* Bible . . . in its history." Thus the legends of the dynasties of Argos and Thebes were mythical for the Greeks in our sense, but were not strictly sacred even in the Greek sense. In Western literature, the overlapping of mythical and sacred is much closer, but even there national history has a particular seriousness. The alternative title of Shakespeare's *Henry VIII*, "All Is True," perhaps indicates a seriousness of this kind, and one that the audience would not have expected from *The Tempest*, even though *The Tempest* has held the stage so much better.

The difference between the mythical and the fabulous is a difference in authority and social function, not in structure. If we were concerned only with structural features we should hardly be able to distinguish them at all. Most of the stories about the accepted divine beings are myths rather than folktales, but structurally this distinction is more one of content than of actual shape. The parallelism in structure between myth and folktale meets us everywhere in literature: an example is the exposed-infant theme of Greek New Comedy, which is not necessarily "derived" from myth but is obviously similar to some myths. There are only so many effective ways of telling a story, and myths and folktales share them without dividing them. But as a distinctive tendency in the social development of literature, myths have two characteristics that folktales, at least in their earlier stages, do not show, or show much less clearly. First, myths stick together to form a mythology, a large interconnected body of narrative that covers all the religious and historical revelation that its society is concerned with, or concerned about. Second, as part of this sticking-together process, myths take root in a specific culture, and it is one of their functions to tell that culture what it is and how it came to be, in their own mythical terms. Thus they transmit a legacy of shared allusion to that culture. Folktales by themselves, at least at first, lead a more nomadic existence. They travel over the world through all the barriers of language: they do not expand into larger structures, but interchange their themes and motifs at random, like the principles of chaos in Milton. But as literature develops, "secular" stories also begin to take root in the culture and contribute to the shared heritage of allusion.

The mythical poet, then, has his material handed him by tradition, whereas the fabulous poet may, up to a point, choose his own plots and characters. Aristophanes produced a distinctive "gimmick" for each of his comedies, and was expected to do so; Sophocles was expected to tell the mythical stories that had been made relevant to the Dionysus cult. Otherwise, the audience could ask, and feel that it had a right to ask, "What has all this to do with Dionysus?" The characters and plots of mythical poets have the resonance of social acceptance about them, and they carry an authority that no writer can command who is merely being what we call "creative." The transmission of tra-

dition is explicit and conscious for the mythical writer
and his audience: the fabulous writer may seem to be
making up his stories out of his own head, but this never
happens in literature, even if the illusion of its happening is
a necessary illusion for some writers. His material comes
from traditions behind him which may have no recognized
or understood social status, and may not be consciously
known to the writer or to his public.

The fact that myths stick together to form a mythology
is clearly shown in an explicitly Christian story, such as
the Barlaam and Josaphat romance, which comes from
about the eighth century. This is said to be a Christianized
version of the story of the Buddha, though there is hardly
enough story for many specific parallels to emerge. Prince
Josaphat is kept in seclusion by his father, who hates
Christianity: the hermit Barlaam gets through to see him
on the pretext that he has a precious jewel to show him.
The jewel turns out to be an interminable sermon in which
Barlaam sets forth the entire structure of Christian mythology from creation to last judgment, with appendices on
the ascetic life, the use of images in ritual, the necessity of
baptism, and the doctrine of the two natures of Christ.
What makes so long a harangue possible—its plausibility
is another matter—is simply the interconnection of the
individual myths in the total Christian mythology: every
concept or doctrine involves all the others. This was similarly the reason for the proverbial length of Puritan sermons, many centuries later. Such sermons were not necessarily digressive or shapeless, but, as in other forms of oral
literature, there were certain mnemonic hooks or couplings leading from one point to the next until everything
that God had in his mind for man had been expounded.

According to the Venerable Bede, this was how English
literature got started with Caedmon. When the harp was

passed around at a feast and guests were expected to take their turns chanting or improvising poetry, Caedmon had to retire to the stable in humiliation. On one such occasion an angel appeared before him and commanded him to sing. The theme suggested to him was the creation, that is, page one of the Bible. Once started on that, there was no stopping Caedmon until he had sung his way through the entire mythological corpus:

He sang of the creation of the world, the origin of the human race, and the whole story of Genesis. He sang of Israel's departure from Egypt, their entry into the land of promise, and many other events of scriptural history. He sang of the Lord's incarnation, passion, resurrection and ascension into heaven, the coming of the Holy Spirit, and the teaching of the apostles. He also made many poems on the terrors of the last judgement, the horrible pains of hell, and the joys of the kingdom of heaven. In addition to these, he composed several others on the blessings and judgements of God, by which he sought to turn his hearers from delight in wickedness and to inspire them to love and do good.

Caedmon was thus doing what the medieval miracle plays were later to do, in huge cyclical sequences that took several days to get through.

But while the difference in social function between myth and fable makes for these differences in characteristics, the identity in structure pulls in the opposite direction. Secular literature, even in the oral stage, also builds up an interconnecting body of stories. Thus *Beowulf*, which is close in its conventions to oral literature, refers parenthetically to other stories about Siegmund, Offa, and Ingeld; and most of the Icelandic Sagas contain allusions or cross-references to other Sagas. Given a slightly different direction of social development, such a body of legend might easily have become mythical in our present sense of the term. Myths stick together because of cultural forces impelling them to do so: these forces are not primarily literary, and mythologies are mainly accepted as structures of belief or social concern rather than imagination. But it is the structure of myths that makes the process possible, and since folktales possess the same kind of structure they can stick together too.

In secular literature, before copyright laws and individual claims to stories are set up, a standard relating to completeness in telling traditional stories seems often to be implied. Others have told this story before, the author gives us to understand, but I'm going to tell it better and more fully, so you won't have to refer to anyone else for missing features. In certain social contexts, such completeness might well become a qualification for passing over from the fabulous to the mythical category, as doubtless happened with the two Homeric poems. The standard of completeness shows the encyclopedic tendency of myth at work in what we are now calling folktale or fable.

The *Beowulf* poet alludes to the story of Offa to identify a contrasting pattern of story: Hygd, the good queen the poet is talking about, reminds him by contrast of Thryth the wife of Offa, who was a bad one. Similarly, an eighteenth-century novelist will tell an inset tale, like the story of the Man on the Hill in *Tom Jones*, which has a narrative movement opposite to that of the main story. The effect of such an inset tale is to establish the main story as one of a category of stories, giving it a broader significance than it would have as an isolated story. As a body of myths expands, it absorbs other stories, especially the stories connected with specific local places and people that are called legends. Thus the great Hebraic myths of the creation, deluge, and exodus expanded to include the legends of the Judges and the prophets Elijah and Elisha. A later process of expansion took in the folktales of Jonah, Ruth, Tobit, Esther, Judith, and Susanna. Christian mythology similarly expanded to include a large body of romance, including many saints' lives and such apocryphal stories as the Harrowing of Hell. Such an absorption of legend marks the political and social ascendancy of a society with a central mythology, as it takes over other areas, and this mythical imperialism is possible because of the structural similarities among all forms of story.

The literature of a polytheistic mythology can emphasize certain cults or even absorb or promote new ones, just as Christianity could use legend to enhance the prestige of a specific saint or shrine. Some of the Greek romancers say that they intend their stories to be an offering to Eros, or a demonstration of that god's power. The conclusion to *The Golden Ass* of Apuleius was evidently among other things a plug for the cult of Isis. The same structural principle may still be used where there is no longer any question of cult. Greene's story *Pandosto*, the main source of Shakespeare's *Winter's Tale*, treats Apollo's oracle at Delphi in a way which would tempt us to assume, if it had been written two thousand years earlier, that it was trying to promote the prestige of that oracle. We are touching here on the relation of imaginative structures to belief or worship: the general principle is that imaginative structures as such are independent of belief, and it makes no difference to the structure whether the implied beliefs are real, pretended, or denounced as demonic, like the religion of the Trojans in Chaucer's *Troilus and Criseyde*.

Just as a mythology may absorb new legendary material, so it may itself cease to carry the sense of superior importance or authority. This happens whenever one culture supersedes another. Classical mythology became fabulous, a branch of secular literature, in Christian times, and biblical mythology, as such, is rapidly becoming fabulous now. Very ancient Near Eastern stories of the creation as the killing of a dragon whose body supplied the material for it, originally mythical, have become fabulous in the Old Testament. Such a use of them, naturally, does not destroy their structural outlines. Similarly, Classical mythology still could, long after it had become fable, be used as a counterpoint to Christian mythology.

The Bible is the supreme example of the way that myths can, under certain social pressures, stick together to make up a mythology. A second look at this mythology shows us that it actually became, for medieval and later centuries, a vast mythological universe, stretching in time from creation to apocalypse, and in metaphorical space from heaven to hell. A mythological universe is a vision of reality in terms of human concerns and hopes and anxieties: it is not a primitive form of science. Unfortunately, human nature being what it is, man first acquires a mythological universe and then pretends as long as he can that it is also the actual universe. All mythological universes are by definition centered on man, therefore the actual universe was also assumed to be centered on man. Some Greek thinkers had realized that the earth went around the sun, but the medieval world ignored them because the geocentric model was more reassuring, at least from the point of view of those who controlled the culture.

The secession of science from the mythological universe is a familiar story. The separating of scientific and mythological space began theoretically with Copernicus, and effectively with Galileo. By the nineteenth century scientific time had been emancipated from mythological time. But in proportion as the mythological universe becomes more obviously a construct, another question arises. We saw that there is no structural principle to prevent the fables of secular literature from also forming a mythology, or even a mythological universe. Is it possible, then, to look at secular stories as a whole, and as forming a single integrated vision of the world, parallel to the Christian and biblical vision? This is the question implied in the "secular scripture" of my title. In the chapters that follow I should like to look at fiction as a total verbal order, with the outlines of an imaginative universe also in it. The Bible is the epic of the creator, with God as its hero. Romance is the structural core of all fiction: being directly descended from folktale, it brings us closer than any other aspect of literature to the sense of fiction, considered as a whole, as the epic of the creature, man's vision of his own life as a quest.

One of my predecessors in the Norton Lectures, J. L. Borges, says, in a little story called "The Gospel According to Mark": "generations of men, throughout recorded time, have always told and retold two stories—that of a lost ship which searches the Mediterranean seas for a dearly loved island, and that of a god who is crucified on Golgotha." The Crucifixion is an episode in the biblical epic: Borges is clearly suggesting that romance, as a whole, provides a parallel epic in which the themes of shipwreck, pirates, enchanted islands, magic, recognition, the loss and regaining of identity, occur constantly, as they do in the last four romances of Shakespeare. Borges is referring to different episodes of the two complete stories, but he puts his finger on an essential structural problem of criticism.

We notice that mythical poets, including Dante and Milton, do not themselves acquire the authority of the myths they treat, unless by accident, or unless, like Homer, they come at the very beginning of a cultural development. The

Devil in Bernard Shaw's *Man and Superman* remarks contemptuously of *Paradise Lost* that to this day every Englishman believes that the whole of Milton's "silly story" is in the Bible. But it is clear that the belief is founded on a cultural misunderstanding, "Englishmen" being more ignorant of what is in the Bible than the Devil can afford to be. If one actually does know the Bible or the teachings of a religion based on it, he has probably not derived his knowledge from the poets. The distinction of mythical and fabulous, in other words, overlaps not only with the distinction of sacred and secular, but with the distinction of true and false, or of what is believed to be true or false.

Myths are usually assumed to be true, stories about what really happened. But truth is not the central basis for distinguishing the mythical from the fabulous: it is a certain quality of importance or authority for the community that marks the myth, not truth as such. The anxiety of society, when it urges the authority of a myth and the necessity of believing it, seems to be less to proclaim its truth than to prevent anyone from questioning it. It aims at consent, including the consent of silence, rather than conviction. Thus the Christian myth of providence, after a battle, is often invoked by the winning side in a way which makes its truth of secondary importance. The storm that wrecked the Spanish Armada was a providential event to the English, but a natural event to the Spaniards. Elizabeth I issued a medal quoting the Psalms, "God breathed with his winds, and they were scattered"; Philip of Spain said to the survivors: "I sent you forth to fight with men, not with the elements."

Shakespeare's Henry V makes it a capital offense to give credit for the victory of Agincourt to anyone but God. The French, whose opinion did not count, would have ascribed it rather to the bitch-goddess Fortune, and some even in the English army—Fluellen, for example—might have agreed with them. But such dissenting voices have to be silenced as long as the excitement of the victory lasts. Similarly, while the battle was going on, it would have been highly injudicious to question the assumption that St. George was supporting the English or, on the other side, St. Denis the French, much less suggest that one saint originated in a pagan folktale and the other in a pious fraud. Yet the first doubt at least might have been defensible theologically, even in the fifteenth century.

Greek critics distinguished verbal structures as true, false, and plastic, or more accurately plasmatic, the presenting of things as they conceivably could be. Truth and falsehood are not literary categories, and are only approximately even verbal ones. For the literary critic, at all events, everything in words is plasmatic, and truth and falsehood represent the directions or tendencies in which verbal structures go, or are thought to go. This leads to a general distinction between serious and responsible literature on the one hand, and the trifling and fantastic on the other. Again, these are not literary categories, or qualities inherent in literary works themselves. They are the primary elements of the social acceptance of or response to literature. Hence what is accepted as serious or dismissed as trifling may vary from one age to another, depending on currents of fashion or cultural attitudes operating for the most part outside literature.

The original criterion of truth is personal: a thing is true because a tradition of sufficient authority, or a person representing that tradition, says or endorses it. Here truth is identified, not so much with the verifiable statement, as with the "existential" statement of supreme importance for the community. This personal standard of truth is normally established under the social conditions of an oral culture, and we notice how the great religious teachers tend to disclaim all connection with writing and confine themselves to the spoken word. Later on, truth tends to be thought of rather as truth of correspondence. A verbal structure describes something, and is called true if it is a satisfactory set of verbal symbols for what it describes. The development of writing throws a heavy emphasis on the descriptive aspect of words, and consequently a writing culture tends to identify truth more and more completely with truth of verbal correspondence.

In proportion as this more rational conception of truth develops, the fabulous acquires the quality of the imaginary, of something admitted not to be true. And because of the structural identity of fable and myth, the word myth, like the words fable and fiction, also takes on a connotation of "not really true." The New Testament uses the word *mythos* in this sense, and urges us to avoid *bebelous mythous*, profane stories. *Mythoi*, or just stories, were what other religions had: what Christians had were *logoi*, true stories. Confronted with this distinction, a literary critic can say only that the structural principles of the two appear to be identical. But if one story is true and another one of the same shape false, the difference between them can only be established by attaching a body of discursive writing to the true story, designed to verify or rationalize its truth.

The same point had struck Plato much earlier. It horrified Plato that the accredited teachers of religion in his day were poets employing myths instead of philosophers employing dialectic. Plato used myths himself a good deal, of course, as has been often enough said since his time. But there appear to be different levels of myth in Plato. On the highest level, myths are illustrations of principles established by dialectic, the instrument of knowledge about the intelligible world. From that knowledge we move up to a myth showing this knowledge in a state of union, the wise man's untroubled vision of reality. We cannot enter into the great myths of creation, reincarnation, or the history of Atlantis which Socrates and Timaeus expound without a preliminary training in philosophy. Such myths are as far as possible removed from the obstacle myths or silly stories which offend our sense of reality and moral decorum, and yet have gained a special authority by tradition. Plutarch says that the gods of whom indecent stories can be told are no gods: it follows that such stories are not true myths. Thus Plato, if I am right about him, makes the distinction between myth and fable as wide as he can get it, one being at the top and the other at the bottom of his vision of reality.

But for Plato knowledge about the intelligible world is also to be used for controlling the masses of people below it, who live by trust in authority. For them, whatever can be formulated as a doctrine, a history, a law, an argument, or a moral principle, and so belongs outside literature, can be illustrated by a story. The story is popular, addresses itself to untutored minds, and so helps to overcome the gap between the rulers who know and the ruled who must believe. The latter, if they do not know what truth is, may have to be lied to. But a myth on this lower level may be a lie and still represent true indoctrination, and true indoctrination is the real social function of literature. Much of what the poets give us, however, is lower-level myth without any relation to true indoctrination, still less to dialectic: this is part of the shadow-knowledge which has no function in Plato's republic.

Similarly, Christianity possessed a body of true myth or revelation, most of it in the Bible. This was distinguished from unauthorized myth by having a large body of conceptual writing attached to it, the doctrinal system of Christian theology. As with Plato, the Christian has to pass through this doctrinal system before he can understand the myths of the Bible. In the nineteenth century Cardinal Newman remarked that the function of scripture was not to teach doctrine but to prove it: this axiom shows how completely the structure of the Bible had been translated into a conceptual system which both replaced and enclosed it. Even the fact that the original data were for the most part stories, as far as their structure is concerned, often came to be resented or even denied. Whatever resisted the translating operation had to be bracketed as a mystery of faith, into which it was as well not to look too closely.

When Christianity came to northern Europe, one of its first tasks was to destroy non-Christian mythology, along with the heroic poetry that could serve as a rallying point for a cultural tradition outside Christianity. Such poetry flourished with great persistence, and as late as 800 Alcuin could warn against listening to it, asking *Quid Hinieldus cum Christo?*—What has the northern hero Ingeld to do with Christ? He was paraphrasing St. Paul, but also echoing the protest of the conservative Athenians: "What has all this to do with Dionysus?" Alcuin spoke for the great majority of those who controlled the art of writing, and they saw to it that we today have only the most fragmentary knowledge of what must have been a very great oral tradition. In doing so they set up, for a new cycle of civilization, much the same model of social response to literature that Plato had used, and passed it on to us. The similarity between biblical myths and the fables of the heathen could be accounted for by the fact that the devil, like man, is a clever mimic.

The Platonic revolution, as transmitted through Christianity, has given us a hierarchy of verbal structures with four main levels in it. On top is the level of high myth, biblical or Platonic, which is not only not literary but cannot be really understood except by those who have passed beyond the need for literature. Next come the serious verbal structures, the nonliterary ones that tell the truth by correspondence about history, religion, ethics, or social life. Below this is the relatively serious literature that reflects their truths and communicates them to the populace in the more agreeable forms of story or rhetorical embellishment. This is the middle ground of myth, in Plato the level where poets may operate by writing hymns to the gods and encomia on virtuous men. Below this is the literature designed only to entertain or amuse, which is out of sight of truth, and should be avoided altogether by serious people.

There are two results of this situation, one positive and constructive, the other negative and obstructive. The positive result was only possible because the rigorously hard line of this attitude did not maintain itself. There were many mitigating factors, like Aristotle's more liberal conception of mimesis, and because of them literature did succeed in gaining a real place in the Christian social order. As its place was essentially secular, the imaginative standards came to be set by the fabulous writers, and the mythical ones had to meet those standards. They got no special advantage, except by accident, from choosing themes to which their society attached special importance. There is said to be an illustration in an early edition of *The Pilgrim's Progress* showing the plays of John Dryden being advertised in Vanity Fair. Bunyan would certainly have thought that his theme, the imitation of Christ in the Christian life, gave his book, whatever its aesthetic merits, a fundamental seriousness that no play of Dryden's could possibly match. Samuel Johnson, Coleridge, perhaps Matthew Arnold, would have agreed with the general principle, without being able to take Bunyan as seriously as Dryden within the category of literature itself. Samuel Johnson says that Pope's *Messiah* is greatly superior to Virgil's Fourth Eclogue, but that this is no credit to Pope, because Pope has derived his poem from an immeasurably superior source, the Book of Isaiah. This statement is nonsense as far as literary criticism is concerned, and Johnson knows that it is nonsense: he is making the statement simply to emphasize the priority of his religious commitments to his literary standards.

The negative results of the Platonic and Christian view, however, are more obvious and important for the subject of romance. Serious literature, according to that view, is addressed to those who have a natural hankering for pleasure, and really want to read just for fun, but can be persuaded to read for instruction as well. It is for this group, according to a principle generally accepted in Elizabethan times, that Classical mythology is intended. The fables of the gods are pleasant enough to entice the more light-minded reader, but when he digests them he will find that they are really wholesome food, that is, moral platitudes. Thus Adlington, in the preface to his translation of Apuleius:

And therefore the poets feigned not their fables in vain, considering that children in time of their first studies are very much allured thereby to proceed to more grave and deep studies . . . By the fable of Actaeon, where it is feigned that when he saw Diana washing herself in a well, he was immediately turned into an hart, and so was slain of his own dogs, may be meant, that when a man casteth his eyes on the vain and soon fading beauty of the world . . . he seemeth to be turned into a brute beast . . . The fall of Icarus is an example to proud and arrogant persons, that weeneth to climb up to the heavens . . . By Phaeton, that unskilfully took in hand to rule the chariot of the sun, are represented those persons which attempt things passing their power and capacity.

We finally come, at the bottom of the hierarchy, to popular literature, or what people read without guidance from their betters. Popular literature has been the object of a constant bombardment of social anxieties for over two thousand years, and nearly the whole of the established critical tradition has stood out against it. The greater part of the reading and listening public has ignored the critics and censors for exactly the same length of time. This is an issue which we shall have to look into, because the bulk of popular literature consists of what I have been calling sentimental romance.

Any serious discussion of romance has to take into account its curiously proletarian status as a form generally disapproved of, in most ages, by the guardians of taste and learning, except when they use it for their own purposes. The close connection of the romantic and the popular runs all through literature. The formulas of New Comedy and Greek romance were demotic and popular formulas, like their counterparts now, treated with condescension by the highbrows, one form of condescension being the writing of such tales themselves, as academics write detective stories today. A similar situation, according to Arthur Waley, appeared in Classical China, which produced some excellent romances although romance was never accepted as a valid form of literature.

Popular literature, the guardians of taste feel, is designed only to entertain: consequently reading it is a waste of time. More closely regarded by anxiety, it turns out to be something far worse than a waste of time. Romance in particular is, we say, "sensational": it likes violent stimulus, and the sources of that stimulus soon become clear to the shuddering censor. The central element of romance is a love story, and the exciting adventures are normally a foreplay leading up to a sexual union. Hence romance appears to be designed mainly to encourage irregular or excessive sexual activity. This may be masturbation, which is the usual model in the minds of those who speak with contempt of "escape" reading, or it may be a form of voyeurism. Most denunciations of popular romance on such grounds, we notice, assume that the pornographic and the erotic are the same thing: this overlooks the important principle that it is the function of pornography to stun and numb the reader, and the function of erotic writing to wake him up.

Throughout the history of culture, not many people have really questioned this Platonic and traditionally Christian framework. In every age it has been generally assumed that the function of serious literature is to produce illustrations of the higher truths conveyed by expository prose. The real social function of literature, in this view, is to persuade the emotions to align themselves with the reason, and so act on the "heart," which perhaps means not so much the pump in the chest as the primary or primitive brain. The disputes are mainly, not about the status of literature, but about how efficient the serious aspect of serious literature is in separating itself from the moral turpitude of mere entertainment.

Every so often a particularly bloody-minded censor denies that there is any separation. In Elizabethan times there was Stephen Gosson, an able and acute writer given his premises, who wrote *The School of Abuse* largely to attack the new threat that popular literature was posing in the theater. Gosson demonstrates that Classical myths were not stories told for the sake of their morals: whether the morals are inserted by the poets themselves or by their readers, the stories in themselves are not instructive but delightful, and therefore detestable. An example of a more liberal view founded on similar premises is the implication in Judge Woolsey's court decision on *Ulysses*, which held that *Ulysses* was serious rather than obscene because its attitude to sex was more nauseating ("emetic") than enticing.

Many literary critics today still have Platonic minds, in the sense that they attach what for them are the real values of literature to something outside literature which literature reflects. This may be scholastic theology or Senecan ethics in one age, Marxist economics or Freudian psychology in another, sociolinguistics or phenomenology in another. Freudian and Marxist critics, of the more orthodox kinds at least, generally subscribe to the Platonic view of literature, and I have been amused to notice, in discussions of my own work, how my proposal to take literature itself as the area of critical investigation, without granting anything else priority to it, causes Freudian and Marxist anxieties to go up like barrage balloons.

In bourgeois society, a good deal of anxiety about popular literature has had a vestigial class motivation. Prohibition was clearly part of an effort to impose a middle-class ethic on a working class who might be alcoholically stimulated to do less work. Similarly, sexual prudery has often been a middle-class reaction to the fact that the pleasures of sex are available to ordinary people, and are therefore, as the proverbial lady says, "much too good for them." Phrases emphasizing the cheapness of popular literature, such as "dime novel," or "penny dreadful," lingered long after inflation had made them archaic, and it was a common assumption, sometimes reflected in legislation, that very expensive books were automatically serious. Such anxieties are no longer much with us, except sporadically, but some of the habits of mind they engendered still are, and account for much of our confusion today about the social function of the humanities. I am aware, of course, that popular literature of various types has recently come in for a good deal of academic processing. I am trying to suggest a literary perspective on it which may help to bring it into the area of literary criticism instead of confining it to linguistics or to the less fashionable suburbs of sociology.

There seem to me to be two ways of looking at popular literature. If by popular literature we mean what a great many people want or think they want to read when they are compelled to read, or stare at on television when they are not, then we are talking about a packaged commodity which an overproductive economy, whether capitalist or socialist, distributes as it distributes food and medicines, in varying degrees of adulteration. Much of it, in our society, is quite as prurient and brutal as its worst enemy could assert, not because it has to be, but because those who write and sell it think of their readers as a mob rather than a community. In such a social context the two chief elements of romance, love and adventure, become simply lust and bloodlust. As in most melodrama, there is often a certain self-righteous rationalization of the tone: this is what we're all involved in, whether we like it or not, etc. But the fact that sex and violence emerge whenever they get a chance does mean that sexuality and violence are central to romance: this is an important cultural fact about it which we shall have to return to.

Popular literature could also mean, however, the literature that demands the minimum of previous verbal experience and special education from the reader. In poetry, this

would include, say, the songs of Bⳑ   ke, the Lucy
lyrics of Wordsworth, ballads and rⳑ   and other
simple forms ranging from some of the soⳡgⳋ d sonnets
of Shakespeare to Emily Dickinson. Much if not most of
this would be very unpopular in the bestseller sense, but it
is the kind of material that should be central in the literary
education of children and others of limited contact with
words. When we apply this conception of the popular to
stories in prose, we find ourselves again close to folktale,
and begin to understand more clearly what the real connection between romance and popular literature is.

The central mythical area is an area of special authority,
which means that people in authority take it over. It
becomes the center also of education, and the literature
based on it thus becomes highly allusive and erudite, these
qualities increasing as the mythology expands into other
cultural areas. *Paradise Lost* is "elite" literature, if it is
understood that I am not using the word in its cliché sense.
It is elite not because it is biblical in its choice of subject,
but because the whole structure of humanist learning, with
biblical and Classical mythology radiating out from it, has
to be brought to bear on the reading and study of the
poem. By contrast, *The Pilgrim's Progress* is, or was,
popular literature, because it assumes only the kind of
understanding of the Christian myth that every English
family with any books or education at all would have possessed in Bunyan's day and for two centuries thereafter.
Pope's *Dunciad* is "elite" literature of a more secular kind,
with its echoes from Classical epic and its dense texture of
personal allusion and of what we call in-jokes. Defoe's
Robinson Crusoe is popular because it demands only the
kind of awareness of the world that, again, an eighteenth-
century Englishman likely to read any book would normally have.

If there is anything to be said for this conception of popular literature, we should be careful not to idealize it as a virtuous resistance to elitism, the poor but honest hero of bourgeois romance who triumphs over his wealthier rival. Popular literature, so defined, is neither better nor worse than elite literature, nor is it really a different kind of literature: it simply represents a different social development of it. The same writer may feel the pull of elite and popular tendencies within himself. The popular helps to diversify our literary experience and prevent any type of literary education from getting a monopoly of it; but as time goes on, popular writers without exception survive by being included in the literary "establishment." Thus Spenser has acquired a reputation as a poet's poet and a storehouse of recondite allusion and allegory; but in his day *The Faerie Queene* was regarded as pandering to a middlebrow appetite for stories about fearless knights and beauteous maidens and hideous ogres and dragons, instead of following the more sober Classical models.

As a rule, popular literature in this sense indicates where the next literary developments are most likely to come from. It was the popular theater, not humanist neo-Classical drama, that pointed the way to Marlowe and Shakespeare; it was the popular Deloney, not the courtly and aristocratic Sidney, who showed what the major future forms of prose fiction were going to be like; it was the popular ballad and broadside and keepsake-book doggerel of the eighteenth century that anticipated the *Songs of Innocence* and the *Lyrical Ballads*. In prose, the popular literature signalizing such new developments has usually taken the form of a rediscovery of the formulas of romance.

The history of literature seems to break down into a series of cultural periods of varying length, each dominated by certain conventions. During these periods, what one distinguished scholar of this university has called the burden of the past increases rapidly in weight and oppressiveness. Writers improve and refine on their predecessors until it seems that no further improvement is possible. Then the conventions wear out, and literature enters a transitional phase where some of the burden of the past is thrown off and popular literature, with romance at its center, comes again into the foreground. This happened with Greek literature after New Comedy, when Greek romance emerged; it happened at the end of the eighteenth century in Britain, when the Gothic romances emerged, and it is happening now after the decline of realistic fiction, as I shall try to explain more fully in the next chapter.

We should note that, if we accept my second definition of popular, the words popular and primitive mean essentially the same thing, except that "popular" has its context in class structure and "primitive" in history. If we define popular literature as what ignorant and vicious people read, the prejudice implied will make it impossible to understand what is going on in literature. Similarly, if we define the primitive only as the chronologically early, we create an illusion of literature gradually improving itself from naked savagery to the decent clothing of accepted cultural values. But actually the primitive is a quality in literature which emerges recurrently as an aspect of the popular, and as indicating also that certain conventions have been exhausted. The Greek romancers, for all their coyness, are more primitive in this sense than Homer or Aeschylus; the Gothic romancers, like many of the poets contemporary with them, are primitive in a way that Pope and Swift are not, and so are the folk singers and science fiction writers of our own day as compared with Eliot or Joyce.

In every period of history certain ascendant values are accepted by society and are embodied in its serious literature. Usually this process includes some form of kidnapped romance, that is, romance formulas used to reflect certain ascendant religious or social ideals. Spenser knew very well what he was doing with his ogres and dragons: he was trying to get imaginative support for the Protestant revolution of his time, both in its insurgent phase, the main subject of Book One of *The Faerie Queene*, and in its authoritarian phase, the main subject of Book Five. At other times popular enjoyment of sexuality or violence is simply gratified or exploited. But something forever excluded from accepted values always gets away, never wholly absorbed even by the greatest literature.

Of Borges' two retold stories, the biblical and the romantic, the biblical story finally ends with the Book of Revelation, in a fairytale atmosphere of gallant angels fighting dragons, a wicked witch, and a wonderful gingerbread city glittering with gold and jewels. But the other story, the ship searching the Mediterranean for a lost island, never seems to come to an end. It may go into the Atlantic looking for happy islands here, or into the Pacific, as in Melville's *Mardi*, or into outer space, journeying to planets so remote that light itself is too slow a vehicle. When we study the great classics of literature, from Homer on, we are following the dictates of common sense, as embodied in the author of Ecclesiastes: "Better is the sight of the eye than the wandering of desire." Great literature is what the eye can see: it is the genuine infinite as opposed to the phony infinite, the endless adventures and endless sexual stimulation of the wandering of desire. But I have a notion that if the wandering of desire did not exist, great literature would not exist either.

There is a line of Pope's which exists in two versions: "A mighty maze of walks without a plan," and "A mighty maze, but not without a plan." The first version recognizes the human situation; the second refers to the constructs of religion, art, and science that man throws up because he finds the recognition intolerable. Literature is an aspect of the human compulsion to create in the face of chaos. Romance, I think, is not only central to literature as a whole, but the area where we can see most clearly that the maze without a plan and the maze not without a plan are two aspects of the same thing.

2

The Context of Romance

2

LITERARY CRITICS HAVE inherited from Aristotle
two principles: one, the conception of art as imitating
nature; the other, the distinction of form and content. In
nonliterary writing, the verbal structure imitates what it
describes in the way that a copy imitates an external
model. In literature, however, the art is the form, and the
nature which the art imitates is the content, so in literature
art imitates nature by containing it internally. This principle is a practical one, and still very useful: one limitation
of it is that it relates only to the work of art as product, as
finished and done with. It is perhaps more natural for us
today to think in terms of continuous process or creative
activity, and for that we need two other conceptions parallel to form and content.

In the context of process, the form becomes something
more like the shaping spirit, the power of ordering which
seems so mysterious to the poet himself, because it often
acts as though it were an identity separate from him. What
corresponds to content is the sense of otherness, the resistance of the material, the feeling that there is something to
be overcome, or at least struggled with. Wallace Stevens
calls these two elements imagination and reality: as often
with Stevens' terminology, the words are used much more

precisely than they appear to be, and I shall adopt them here.

The imagination, then, is the constructive power of the mind, the power of building unities out of units. In literature the unity is the *mythos* or narrative; the units are metaphors, that is, images connected primarily with each other rather than separately with the outer world. "Reality," for Stevens, is whatever the imagination works with that is not itself. Left to itself, the imagination can achieve only a facile pseudo-conquest of its own formulas, meeting no resistance from reality. The long-standing association between the words imagination and fancy may suggest that the imaginative, by itself, tends to be fantastic or fanciful. But actually, what the imagination, left to itself, produces is the rigidly conventionalized. In folktales, plot-themes and motifs are predictable enough to be counted and indexed; improvised drama, from *commedia dell'arte* to guerrilla theater, is based on formulas with a minimum of variables. Anyone recording, or reading about, reveries, daydreams, or conscious sexual fantasies must be struck by the total absence in such things of anything like real fantasy. They are formulaic, and the formulaic unit, of phrase or story, is the cornerstone of the creative imagination, the simplest form of what I call an archetype.

In the course of struggling with a world which is separate from itself, the imagination has to adapt its formulaic units to the demands of that world, to produce what Aristotle calls the probable impossibility. The fundamental technique used is what I call displacement, the adjusting of formulaic structures to a roughly credible context. A friend of mine, at the beginning of his teaching career, was faced with teaching a "creative writing" course to students of very limited literary experience. One of his devices was to give them a Grimm fairy tale and tell them to displace it, turning it into a plausible story in which every detail of the original would be accounted for. A literary example of such a technique is Ibsen's *Vikings at Helgeland*, a displacement of the Sigurd saga. Here Fafnir the dragon has become a tame bear, the changing of shapes in the original is accounted for by the heroine's being slightly drunk, and so on. Artificial displacements of this kind are useful mainly for practice pieces; but it is clear even from this example that realistic displacement is closely related to parody.

In the fiction-writing of the last four or five centuries there has been a kind of reversible shuttle moving between imagination and reality, as Stevens uses those words. One direction is called "romantic," the other "realistic." The realistic tendency moves in the direction of the representational and the displaced, the romantic tendency in the opposite direction, concentrating on the formulaic units of myth and metaphor. At the extreme of imagination we find the themes and motifs of folktale, elements of the process that Coleridge distinguished as fancy, and described as "a mode of memory" playing with "fixities and definites." At the extreme of realism comes what is often called "naturalism," and at the extreme of that the shaping spirit wanders among documentary, expository, or reminiscent material, unable to find a clear narrative line from a beginning to an end.

Problems of design, of composition and balance and contrast, are obviously as central in the verbal arts as they are in music or painting. They appear in the rhetorical texture, an obvious example being the antithetical structure that we find in Hebrew parallelism, the Latin elegiac, and the English heroic couplet. They appear in the ballet-like couplings and intertwinings of characters in Goethe's *Elective Affinities* or Henry James' *Golden Bowl;* and they appear in contrapuntal plots like the story of Gloucester in *King Lear*. Characters occupy the *designed* time and space of their creators; they may as logically end their fictional lives at marriage as at death; their paths may cross in sheer "coincidence." The more undisplaced the story, the more sharply the design stands out. Later on we shall refer to Carlo Gozzi, the eighteenth-century Italian dramatist who is useful to a study of romance because he writes undisplaced fairy tales full of magic and metamorphosis. We are not surprised to find that it was Gozzi who maintained that the entire range of dramatic possibilities could be reduced to thirty-six basic situations. The inference for us is that even the most contrived and naive romantic plot, even the most impossibly black-and-white characterization, may still give us some technical insight into the way that stories get told.

The romantic tendency is antirepresentational, and so is parallel to the development of abstract or primitive movements in painting. Critics of painting have learned to examine such pictures on their own terms; critics of fiction have to learn to look at romances, with all their nonrepresentational plots and characters, equally on their own terms. Many Victorian critics of painting demanded anecdotal pictures, because their frame of reference was literary, and so they felt that if a picture were just a picture there would be nothing to say about it. Many literary critics, even yet, are in the same position when confronted with a romance which is "just a story."

When the novel was established in the eighteenth century, it came to a reading public familiar with the formulas of prose romance. It is clear that the novel was a realistic displacement of romance, and had few structural features peculiar to itself. *Robinson Crusoe, Pamela, Tom Jones,* use much the same general structure as romance, but adapt that structure to a demand for greater conformity to ordinary experience. This displacement gave the novel's relation to romance, as I suggested a moment ago, a strong element of parody. It would hardly be too much to say that realistic fiction, from Defoe to Henry James, is, when we look at it as a form of narrative technique, essentially parody-romance. Characters confused by romantic assumptions about reality, who emphasize the same kind of parody, are central to the novel: random examples include Emma Bovary, Anna Karenina, Lord Jim, and Isabel Archer.

The supreme example of the realistic parody of romance is of course *Don Quixote*, which signalized the death of one kind of fiction and the birth of another kind. But the tradition of parody can be traced all through the history of the novel, up to and beyond *Ulysses*, and extends to many novelists who have been thought to be still too close to romance. Thus Fielding's *Joseph Andrews* began as a parody of *Pamela*, and Jane Austen's *Northanger Abbey* is a parody of Gothic romance. The sketches that Jane Austen produced in her teens are nearly all burlesques of popular romantic formulas. And yet, if we read *Pride and Prejudice* or *Emma* and ask the first question about it, which is: what is Jane Austen doing: what is it that drives her pen from one corner of the page to the other, the answer is of course that she is telling a story. The story is the soul of her writing, to use Aristotle's metaphor, the end for which all the words are put down. But if we concentrate on the shape of her stories, we are studying something that brings her much closer to her romantic colleagues, even to the writers of the horrid mysteries she parodied. Her characters are believable, yet every so often we become aware of the tension between them and the outlines of the story into which they are obliged to fit. This is particularly true of the endings, where the right men get married to the right women, although the inherent unlikelihood of these unions has been the main theme of the story. All the adjustments are made with great skill, but the very skill shows that form and content are not quite the same thing: they are two things that have to be unified.

The Waverley novels of Scott mark the absorption of realistic displacement into romance itself. Scott begins his preface to *Waverley* by outlining a number of facile romance formulas that he is *not* going to follow, and then stresses the degree of reality that his story is to have. His hero Waverley is a romantic hero, proud of his good looks and education, but, like a small-scale Don Quixote, his romantic attitude is one that confirms the supremacy of real life. He is over-impressionable, and his loves and loyalties are alike immature. If not really what Scott later called him, "a sneaking piece of imbecility," he is certainly in the central parody-romance tradition of characterization. Parody enters the structure of many other semiromantic novels, though sometimes, as in the later novels of Dickens, it appears to be largely unconscious. In *Little Dorrit* and *Our Mutual Friend* the romantic element, a sprawling octopus of a plot involving disguise, conspiracy, mystery, suspense, and violence, which we can hardly follow at the time and cannot remember afterwards, seems to be almost an anti-narrative. Some features of *Ulysses*, such as the parody of popular female fiction in the "Nausicaa" episode, are similar, and indicate that the real affinities of *Ulysses* are with the past, the tradition stretching from Defoe of which it seems a kind of swan song.

The association of parody and displacement is particularly clear in the many stories, from Mrs. Radcliffe in the eighteenth century to certain types of detective fiction in our day, in which the reader's interest in some fantastic or supernatural situation is worked up, only to be deflated again with a commonplace explanation. In Scott's *Anne of Geierstein* the heroine engages in a certain amount of moonlight flitting, and it is suggested that she is descended from a fairy or elemental spirit, and has acquired by this heredity the ability to transport herself through space without the usual physical movements. A long inset tale is told about her grandmother to lend emotional weight to this suggestion; but eventually everything she does is explained on more or less plausible grounds. The implication in such a device is that fairy tales are for children: the mature reader will want and expect a more matter-of-fact account. The fantasy here is introduced because the action of *Anne of Geierstein* takes place in the fifteenth century, and such fantasy illustrates the kind of superstitions that people at that time had. However, the real effect of the device is to put the undisplaced and displaced versions of the same event side by side. Its significance, then, is not in any child-and-adult value judgment about beliefs, but in the fact that undisplaced versions present the narrative structure more abstractly, just as a cubist or primitive painting would present the geometrical forms of its images more directly than straight representation would do.

As soon as the novel established itself as a respectable literary medium, critics promptly assimilated it to the old Platonic-Christian framework, as described in the previous chapter. The serious literary artists who tell stories in prose, according to this view, also tell us something about the life of their times, and about human nature as it appears in that context, while doing so. Below them comes romance, where the story is told primarily for the sake of the story. This kind of writing is assumed to be much more of a commercial product, and the romancer is considered to have compromised too far with popular literature. Popular literature itself is obviously still in the doghouse.

This means that what gives a novelist moral dignity is

not the story he tells, but a wisdom and insight brought to bear on the world outside literature, and which he has managed to capture within literature. This is what distinguishes George Eliot from Marie Corelli, Joseph Conrad from John Buchan, D. H. Lawrence from Elinor Glyn. All through the nineteenth century and our own there had also been a flourishing development of romance and fantasy, in Wilkie Collins, Bulwer-Lytton, Lewis Carroll, William Morris, and others. Some of these writers were immensely popular in their day, and a few, like Lewis Carroll, have never lost their popularity. But they do not seem to fit the history of fiction as defined by the great realists: they are simply other writers. On the boundary of serious fiction and romance are Scott and Dickens, whose reputations have oscillated a good deal between the two ranks. The setting of *Waverley*, we notice, is a genuine historical event, the 1745 rebellion, and the book is equipped with footnotes indicating an essential mark of literary seriousness, the ability to read nonliterary documents. But Scott came finally to be regarded as too much of a romancer to be worthy of close study. Dickens fared rather better: he too was darkly suspected of being a mere entertainer, but he had obvious social concerns, and besides, he wrote *Hard Times*, a novel so dull that he must surely have had some worthy nonliterary motive for producing it.

The prevailing conception of serious fiction is enshrined in the title of F. R. Leavis' book *The Great Tradition*, a study of George Eliot, Henry James, and Joseph Conrad which assumes that these writers are central in a hierarchy of realistic novelists extending roughly from Defoe to D. H. Lawrence. The assumption seems reasonable, yet when empires start building walls around themselves it is a sign that their power is declining, and the very appearance of such a title indicates a coming change of fashion on the part of both writers and readers. As soon as a defensive wall is in place, the movements of the barbarians on the frontiers, in this case the readers of romance, Westerns, murder mysteries, and science fiction, begin to take on greater historical importance. These movements assumed a more definite shape after the appearance of Tolkien's *Lord of the Rings* in the mid-fifties. On the T. S. Eliot principle that every writer creates his own tradition, the success of Tolkien's book helped to show that the tradition behind it, of George MacDonald and Lewis Carroll and William Morris, was, if not "the great" tradition, a tradition nonetheless. It is a tradition which interests me rather more than Tolkien himself ever did, but for a long time I was in a minority in my tastes. Over twenty years ago, in the remotest corner of a secondhand bookshop, I picked up a cheap reprint of William Morris' *The Roots of the Mountains*. The bookseller remarked that the two little green volumes had been sitting on his shelves since the day he opened his shop in 1913. Fortunately he had some other stock that moved faster, but if the shop is still there it is probably featuring paperback reprints of William Morris romances in a series which, though still cautiously labeled "adult fantasy," seems to be finding its public.

The change of taste in favor of romance raises a good many questions about the validity of some common critical assumptions about fiction which have been fostered by the prestige of a displaced and realistic tradition. There is still a strong tendency to avoid problems of technique and design and structure in fiction, and to concentrate on what the book talks about rather than on what it actually presents. It is still not generally understood either that "reality" in literature cannot be presented at all except within the conventions of literary structure, and that those conventions must be understood first. To give an example of what I mean:

Pirandello's *Six Characters in Search of an Author*

claims to be, at least in its closing scene, a parable of the relation of fiction to reality. Now we notice that one recurring theme in romance is the theme of incest, very often of father and daughter. In the Apollonius story, retold by Gower and the basis of Shakespeare's *Pericles*, we are first introduced to the wicked king Antiochus, who is sexually connected with his daughter. Apollonius himself, or Pericles, the hero of the story, also acquires a daughter whom he loses, who is sold to a brothel, who meets him when he does not know who she is. In short, father-daughter incest keeps hanging over the story as a possibility until nearly the end. This part of the Apollonius story is said to be derived from a lost play of Euripides in which a father unknowingly buys his daughter as a slave, and in which the threat of incest must have been more imminent. In Pirandello the inner play of the six characters, representing reality, is a gloomy melodrama in which at the crucial scene a man enters a brothel and becomes involved with a girl who turns out to be—guess what—his own daughter. The play shows us nothing at all about the relation of fiction to reality: what it shows us is that some conventions of storytelling are more obsessive than others.

In the general area of romance we find highly stylized patterns like the detective story, which are so conventionalized as to resemble games. We expect each game of chess to be different, but we do not want the conventions of the game itself to alter, or to see a chess game in which the bishops move in straight lines and the rooks diagonally. Whether we consider detective stories worth reading or not depends on our willingness to accept the convention. Edmund Wilson, for example, refused to accept the convention, and remarked that readers of detective stories were obviously neurotics trying to attach an inflated importance to a pointless activity. Now if we do find wit, lively plotting, vivid characterization, or cogent social comment in detective stories—and it is not so difficult to find such things—we should appreciate the author's ingenuity in getting good writing into so ritualistic a form. The right next step for criticism, it seems to me, is not to assume that there is a difference in value between detective fiction and other types of fiction, but to realize that all fiction is conventionalized, and that it is equally a *tour de force* of ingenuity to get good characterization and social insight into a story as complicated as *Tom Jones* or *Emma*, both of which also contain mysteries impelling us to continue reading until we reach the "solution."

It will have occurred to you already that this "romantic" and "realistic" contrast is a nineteenth-century one, and that even in the nineteenth century it will not always work: it will not work with Balzac, for instance. But the prestige of "realism" in the nineteenth century reflected the prevailing fashions of that culture, nearly all of which emphasized some form of correspondence, the paralleling of mental structures with something in the outer world. It was an age of representational painting and realistic fiction, and of analogical, or, as I generally call it, allegorical criticism, approaching works of literature as historical or psychological documents. The reason for such an emphasis in criticism is that the more displaced a work of fiction is, the easier it is to see it in terms of its social function rather than its structure. When we start to read Zola or Dreiser, our first impulse is to ask, not what kind of a story is being told, but what is being said about the society that the story is "reflecting."

The beginning of a new kind of criticism is marked by Oscar Wilde's *The Decay of Lying*, which explains very lucidly that, as life has no shape and literature has, literature is throwing away its one distinctive quality when it tries to imitate life. It follows for Wilde that what is called realism does not create but can only record things on a subcreative level:

M. Zola sits down to give us a picture of the Second Empire. Who cares for the Second Empire now? It is out of date. Life goes faster than Realism, but Romanticism is always in front of Life.

Wilde was clearly the herald of a new age in literature, which would take another century or so to penetrate the awareness of critics. He is looking forward to a culture which would use mythical and romantic formulas in its literature with great explicitness, making once more the essential discovery about the human imagination, that it is always a form of "lying," that is, of turning away from the descriptive use of language and the correspondence form of truth. The nineteenth century was also an age that threw up such philosophical schools as "idealism" and (in a different context) "realism," which may be described as two sets of reasons for feeling confident about the adequacy of words to represent external reality. Twentieth-century literature and painting are part of the same cultural movement that in philosophy has shifted the center of interest back to the linguistic structure itself, after destroying much of our old naive confidence that words have an unlimited ability to represent things outside themselves.

Nineteenth-century writers of romance, or of fiction which is close to romance in its technique, sometimes speak in their prefaces and elsewhere of the greater "liberty" that they feel entitled to take. By liberty they mean a greater designing power, especially in their plot structures. Some time back I dropped the word "coincidence," and the word is worth pausing a moment on. In displaced or realistic fiction the author tries to avoid coincidence. That is, he tries to conceal his design, pretending that things are happening out of inherent probability. The convention of avoiding coincidence is so strong that we often say such things as "if this happened in a book, nobody would believe it." In *Jane Eyre* the heroine, in flight from Rochester's proposal to make her his mistress, wanders into the world at random, and is eventually taken in by the only family in England with which she has a previous connection unknown to herself. The odds against the inherent probability of this are so vast that we say, mildly, that it is a farfetched coincidence. In ordinary life a coincidence is a piece of design for which we can find no practical use. Hence, though coincidences certainly happen in ordinary life, they have no point there except to suggest that life at times is capable of forming rudimentary literary designs, thereby seeming to be almost on the point of making sense. Those disposed to believe in providence, that is, a power that shapes our rough-hewn ends into more symmetrical forms, generally comic ones, are often inspired by such a coincidence to express their belief. "Seems like it was sort of meant, like," to quote an example I once overheard. Doubtless Charlotte Brontë had her views about providence too, even if we can see no providence in this case except her desire to tell her story without inhibitions.

In realism the attempt is normally to keep the action horizontal, using a technique of causality in which the characters are prior to the plot, in which the problem is normally: "given these characters, what will happen?" Romance is more usually "sensational," that is, it moves from one discontinuous episode to another, describing things that happen to characters, for the most part, externally. We may speak of these two types of narrative as the "hence" narrative and the "and then" narrative. Most realistic fiction, down to about the middle of the nineteenth century, achieved some compromise between the two, but after the rise of a more ironic type of naturalism the "hence" narrative gained greatly in prestige, much of which it still retains.

The question of how far any real logic or causality is involved in a "hence" narrative is doubtless very complicated, but fortunately does not concern us. We often use the word "logic" to mean the continuity of an emotional drive, as when a man despairing of justice in this life is forced by "logic" to believe in another one. The literary critic deals only with rhetoric, and one of the functions of rhetoric is to present an *illusion* of logic and causality. On the other side, a very clear example of an "and then" narrative is the Apollonius story, which I have already referred to. Apollonius is a suitor to the daughter of king Antiochus, who, we remember, lives in incest with her. Antiochus presents him with a riddle setting forth the situation. If Apollonius fails to solve it he must die, according to the conventions in such matters; if he succeeds he must die anyway because the secret will be out. Not very logical, that is, not very rhetorically convincing as an illusion of logic, but, as Coleridge remarks about the Arabian Nights, the abandoning of such logic has its own fascination, and in any case all we want to know is what will happen next. Well, Apollonius does solve it, whereupon Antiochus, for unstated reasons, not impossibly connected with the need to have something to come next, gives him a respite of thirty days.

Apollonius goes to Tarsus, where he is warned of the danger to his life by a friend he meets there. In a displaced or probable story this would mean that the guilty secret of Antiochus was already well known throughout his world. Apollonius learns that the Tarsians cannot protect him

Tobit sort of follows another = same novel [?]

against Antiochus because they are starving to death in a famine, whereupon he goes back to his own domain, the city of Tyre, and returns with a hundred thousand pecks of grain to feed Tarsus. However, he still has to avoid the vengeance of Antiochus. Antiochus then dies, and Apollonius, along with the reader, are told for the first time that Apollonius is the heir to Antiochus' kingdom. Instead of entering on his inheritance, however, Apollonius goes to Egypt, where he stays fourteen years. He loses his daughter, who after a very rough time is eventually reunited with him. He has also lost his wife at sea, and is finally told in a dream, doubtless sent by a god who is getting tired of the story, to go to Ephesus and expound his adventures to the chief priestess in the temple of Diana there. She being his lost wife, that fixes that up. Some of the gaps in this story, including the credibility gaps, may be the result of trying to keep the action moving at all costs; but there are other places, such as the journey to Egypt, where the storyteller seems to abandon, even to avoid, the line of direct action.

In any case the Apollonius story is not just a series of "and thens": it drives us on toward a conclusion which restates the theme of the opening. At the beginning Apollonius encounters a king who is living in incest with his daughter, so that his daughter is also his wife: at the end Apollonius himself is a prince united with his lost wife and daughter. The story proceeds toward an end which echoes the beginning, but echoes it in a different world. The beginning is the demonic parody of the end, and the action takes place on two levels of experience. This principle of action on two levels, neither of them corresponding very closely to the ordinary world of experience, is essential to romance, and shows us that romance presents a *vertical* perspective which realism, left to itself, would find it very difficult to achieve. The realist, with his sense of logical and horizontal continuity, leads us to the end of his story; the romancer, scrambling over a series of disconnected episodes, seems to be trying to get us to the top of it.

This vertical perspective partly accounts for the curious polarized characterization of romance, its tendency to split into heroes and villains. Romance avoids the ambiguities of ordinary life, where everything is a mixture of good and bad, and where it is difficult to take sides or believe that people are consistent patterns of virtue or vice. The popularity of romance, it is obvious, has much to do with its simplifying of moral facts. It relieves us from the strain of trying to be fair-minded, as we see particularly in melodrama, where we not only have outright heroism and villainy but are expected to take sides, applauding one and hissing the other. In the context of play, of which more in a moment, this moral polarizing provides the same kind of emotional release that a war does, when we are encouraged to believe in our own virtue and the viciousness of the enemy. In the university disturbances of a few years ago, the exuberance in creating simple melodramas out of very mixed-up situations reminded many people, with some justification from a critic's point of view, of similar romance conventions on television.

If we ask why such a story as the Apollonius romance was so popular, one answer is that a sequence of archetypes, traditional fictional formulas or building blocks, has an interest in itself, however poor the logic or "hence" narrative connecting them may be. Thus in the Tarsus episode, where Apollonius finds the city starving, returns to Tyre, and comes back with ships loaded with grain, the archetype is that of the young hero coming over the sea as an image of fertility and the renewal of the food supply, the same one that lies behind the St. George story. The lack of plausibility does not matter, because the formula holds the attention like a bright light or color.

If we further ask why Shakespeare used the Apollonius romance, not only for an early and experimental comedy, but for one of his final plays, we are up against a more central problem of criticism. Ben Jonson called *Pericles* a "mouldy tale," and his view has been often echoed by others, including by implication Shakespeare himself, who almost goes out of his way in *The Winter's Tale* to emphasize the naive and corny nature of his plot. In most traditional tales that are reworked by great writers, what is traditional is the "and then" sequence of events, and the writer himself supplies his own "hence" connective tissue. *Pericles*, however, seems to be a deliberate experiment in presenting a traditional archetypal sequence as nakedly and baldly as possible. Perhaps literature as a whole, like so many works of literature, ends in much the same place that it begins. The profoundest kind of literary experience, the kind that we return to after we have, so to speak, seen everything, may be very close to the experience of a child listening to a story, too spellbound to question the narrative logic.

There are other dramas—Goethe's *Faust*, for example—which have been criticized for lack of "unity," meaning continuity or "hence" narrative, but might display a good deal more coherence to critics able to see them as archetypal sequences. Another fiction writer who specializes in setting down the traditional formulas of storytelling without bothering with much narrative logic is Edgar Allan Poe. This fact, along with the ascendancy of realism, accounts for the curiously schizophrenic quality of Poe's critical reception. There have been no lack of people to say that Poe is fit only for immature minds; yet Poe was the major influence on one of the subtlest schools of poetry that literature has ever seen. Similarly, it is clear that of all Shakespeare's plays, one that affected T. S. Eliot very powerfully was the "mouldy tale" of *Pericles*. This is explicit in "Marina," but I think the influence of Shakespeare's Phoenician sailor goes far beyond that poem. The episodic structure of *Pericles* may remind us of the theme of time in *Four Quartets*, the conception of human life itself as much more a series of "and thens" than a continuous narrative, and where reality is more in the up-and-down perspective than in the horizontal one.

In *Pericles* the discontinuity of the action forces us to see the vertical shape of the whole story, but the same shape is still there in more continuous actions. Very highly concentrated romance, say *The Tempest* or the third book of *The Faerie Queene*, often shows us a carefully arranged hierarchy of characters, which in *The Tempest* ranges from Prospero at the top to the "three men of sin" at the bottom. One might rank these three in a sub-hierarchy with Antonio as low man, as Auden appears to be doing in *The Sea and the Mirror*. Such stage directions as "Prospero on the top, invisible," may even suggest some incorporating of this hierarchy into the staging of the play. The general principle is that the higher up we are, the more clearly we can see the bottom of the action as a demonic parody of the top. Thus in Dante's *Purgatorio*, after Dante has climbed the whole of the mountain and got rid of all his sins, he sees the consolidated demonic vision of the *Inferno*, in its biblical form of Beast and Whore. Similarly, Gower tells the Apollonius story because the theme of incest makes it an illustration of the seventh deadly sin of lechery, the one that medieval writers and preachers left to the end as the most interesting. Doubtless for Gower it would be the reading of the whole story through to the end that would enable the reader to see incest as sinful rather than merely entertaining.

The characterization of romance is really a feature of its mental landscape. Its heroes and villains exist primarily to symbolize a contrast between two worlds, one above the level of ordinary experience, the other below it. There is, first, a world associated with happiness, security, and peace; the emphasis is often thrown on childhood or on an "innocent" or pre-genital period of youth, and the images are those of spring and summer, flowers and sunshine. I shall call this world the idyllic world. The other is a world of exciting adventures, but adventures which involve separation, loneliness, humiliation, pain, and the threat of more pain. I shall call this world the demonic or night world. Because of the powerful polarizing tendency in romance, we are usually carried directly from one to the other.

It looks, therefore, as though romance were simply replacing the world of ordinary experience by a dream world, in which the narrative movement keeps rising into wish fulfillment or sinking into anxiety and nightmare. To some extent this is true. The realistic tendency seeks for its material, or, more accurately, for analogies to its material, in the world of waking consciousness; the up-and-down movement of romance is an indication that the romancer is finding analogies to his material also in a world where we "fall" asleep and wake "up." In many works of fiction reality is equated with the waking world and illusion with dreaming or madness or excessive subjectivity. Examples range from *Don Quixote* to Jane Austen, but, as these examples make clear, such a standard marks the ascendancy of realism. The romancer, *qua* romancer, does not accept these categories of reality and illusion. Both his idyllic and his demonic worlds are a mixture of the two, and no commonsense assumptions that waking is real and dreaming unreal will work for romance. The passengers on the wrecked ship in *The Tempest*, though never at any moment quite sure whether they are waking or dreaming, go on with their habitual reactions. When Antonio and Sebastian plot to murder Alonso, they are following the directives of *Realpolitik*: this is the kind of thing you do in the "real" world if you want to get ahead. Ferdinand, watching the masque of spirits enacting Prospero's fancies, assumes that what he is seeing is an illusion, however delightful. Both are right in a way, but not in the play's way: the standards of reality and illusion that the play presents are the opposite of these.

What there does seem to be is some connection between illusion and anxiety or apprehension, and between reality and serenity; between illusion and tyranny and between reality and freedom; between illusion and the absence of identity, "When no man was his own," as Gonzalo says, and between reality and the possession or recovery of it. Reality for romance is an order of existence most readily associated with the word identity. Identity means a good many things, but all its meanings in romance have some connection with a state of existence in which there is nothing to write about. It is existence before "once upon a time," and subsequent to "and they lived happily ever after." What happens in between are adventures, or collisions with external circumstances, and the return to identity is a release from the tyranny of these circumstances. Illusion for romance, then, is an order of existence that is best called alienation. Most romances end happily, with a return to the state of identity, and begin with a departure from it. Even in the most realistic stories there is usually some trace of a plunge downward at the beginning and a bounce upward at the end. This means that most romances exhibit a cyclical movement of descent into a night world and a return to the idyllic world, or to some symbol of it like a marriage: this cyclical movement is what the remainder of this book will try to explore in more detail.

According to Aristotle (expanding the very elliptical argument slightly), two types of human actions are imitated in words. The historian imitates human actions or *praxeis* as such: everything "practical" that man does, from kings planning wars to peasants digging their fields, may be material for history. There are other types of action which are symbolic and representative of human life in a more universal perspective, and which the poet is more interested in. For these actions the best term is ritual. Religious services, weddings and funerals, convocations and Norton lectures, parades and tournaments, parties and balls and receptions, games and sporting events of all kinds, centennial celebrations, are rituals in this sense. Rituals, like myths, begin in the stage of society described by the term *religio:* they are symbolic acts of social cohesion in which the acts that we think of as specifically "religious" are not yet clearly differentiated from others. We said that in romance as a whole neither the waking world nor the dream world is the real one, but that reality and illusion are both mixtures of the two. Similarly, ritual is a conscious waking act, but there is always something sleepwalking about it: something consciously being done, and something else unconsciously meant by what is being done.

One of the major nonliterary social functions of myth is to explain or rationalize or provide the source of authority for rituals. We do this now, the myth says, because once upon a time, etc. The ritual is, so to speak, the epiphany of the myth, the manifestation or showing forth of it in action. In literature itself the *mythos* or narrative of fiction, more especially of romance, is essentially a verbal imitation of ritual or symbolic human action. This is clearest in drama, where the presentation of the play is itself ritualistic, and still clearer in highly romantic forms of drama, such as Peele's *Old Wives' Tale* or *Mucedorus*, or, once again, the last plays of Shakespeare or Ibsen. The decline of realism in our day has gone along with the rise of the film, with its unprecedented power of presenting symbolic action.

A drama is described as a play: play is normally the opposite of work, and Ben Jonson was subjected to some ridicule when he published his plays under the title of *The Works of Ben Jonson*. The difference between the practical actions studied by historians and the ritual actions expressed in literature might be called, perhaps, actions of work and actions of play, keeping in mind the fact that play, as Huizinga points out in *Homo Ludens*, is not necessarily either enjoyable or free from the sense of obligation. Work is purposeful, directed to an external end; ritual, except for its connection with magic, is self-contained and expressive. Work is done in the actual environment; ritual is enacted within what I have called a mythological universe.

Narrative forms have to depend more than drama does on descriptions of rituals: hence the long accounts of tournaments in chivalric romance, singing matches in pastorals like Sidney's *Arcadia*, the highly stylized scenes of courtship in love stories, and the like. The same punctuating of the narrative by social ritual occurs in realistic fiction too, ranging from the court scenes in *War and Peace* to the reception that triggers off the tremendous meditative explosion in the last volume of Proust. But in romance, essentially the whole human action depicted in the plot is ritualized action. The ritualizing of action is what makes possible the technique of summarized narrative that we find in the "and then" stories of romance, which can move much more quickly than realism can from one episode to another.

In a medieval chivalric romance the jousts and tournaments, the centripetal movement of knights to Arthur's or Charlemagne's court and their dispersal out from it into separate quests, the rescued damsels and beloved ladies, the giants and helpful or perilous beasts, all form a ritualized action expressing the ascendancy of a horse-riding aristocracy. They also express that aristocracy's dreams of its own social function, and the idealized acts of protection and responsibility that it invokes to justify that function. The same thing is true of all ages of romance, from the Cinderella and industrious-apprentice romances of bourgeois aggressiveness to the adventure stories of Rider Haggard and John Buchan and Rudyard Kipling which incorporate the dreams of British imperialism. This is the process of what we called "kidnapping" romance, the absorbing of it into the ideology of an ascendant class.

When we look at social acts as rituals, we become at once aware of their close relation to a good deal of what goes on within the mind. Anyone reading, say, William James' *Varieties of Religious Experience* must be impressed by the extraordinary skill with which many people arrange their lives in the form of romantic or dramatic ritual, in a way which is neither wholly conscious nor wholly unconscious, but a working alliance of the two. William James takes us into psychology, and with Freud and Jung we move into an area where the analogy to quest romance is even more obvious. In a later development, Eric Berne's "transactional" therapy, we are told that we take over "scripts" from our parents which it is our normal tendency to act out as prescribed and invariable rituals, and that all possible forms of such scripts can be found in any good collection of folktales. Romance often deliberately descends into a world obviously related to the human unconscious, and we are not surprised to find that some romances, George MacDonald's *Phantastes*, for example, are psychological quests carried out in inner space. Such inner space is just as much of a "reality," in Wallace Stevens' use of the word, as the Vanity Fair of Thackeray: Vanity Fair itself, after all, is simply a social product of the illusions thrown up by the conflicts within this inner consciousness. When we look back at the Cistercian developments of Arthurian legend, with their stories of Galahad the pure and his quest for the Holy Grail, we see that an identity between individual and social quests has always been latent in romance.

When psychology enters this area, it is concerned mainly with the defensive devices that people use in trying to strengthen the barriers between the waking consciousness and other parts of the mind. That is, it is concerned with the individual counterpart of what I have just called kidnapped romance, the constant effort to keep the romantic thrust of sexuality and wish fulfillment under the control of the status quo. In relation to the actual world, Freud's picture of the ego as a sort of Poor Tom, fighting for its life against an id and a superego and any number of other foul fiends biting it in the behind is perhaps as good as any. For the actual world, as such, keeps dreaming and waking, play and work, in a continuous antithesis: each takes its turn in dominating our interests, yet remains separate from the other. But man lives in two worlds, the world of nature and the world of art that he is trying to build out of nature. The world of art, of human culture and civilization, is a creative process informed by a vision. The focus of this vision is indicated by the polarizing in romance between the world we want and the world we don't want. The process goes on in the actual world, but the vision which informs it is clear of that world, and must be kept unspotted from it. If it is not, ritual is degraded into compulsive magic and the creative energy of the poet into the anxieties of the kind of social concern that has been called, very accurately, the treason of the clerks.

In English literature, perhaps the purest evocations of the idyllic world are Milton's *L'Allegro* and *Il Penseroso*, where the alternating rhythm of ritual and dream, the need to experience as part of a community and the need to experience as a withdrawn individual, have been transformed into complementary creative moods. We notice that L'Allegro spends a good deal of his time listening to the tales of naive romance, and Il Penseroso a corresponding amount of time reading sentimental romance, "where more is meant than meets the ear." The phrase expresses the haunting sense of what is often called allegory in romance, but it seems to me that the word allegory here is misleading: I should prefer some such phrase as "symbolic spread," the sense that a work of literature is expanding into insights and experiences beyond itself. The symbolic spread of realism tends to go from the individual work of fiction into the life around it which it reflects: this can be accurately called allegorical. The symbolic spread of a romance tends rather to go into its literary context, to other romances that are most like it in the conventions adopted. The sense that more is meant than meets the ear in romance comes very largely from the reverberations that its familiar conventions set up within our literary experience, like a shell that contains the sound of the sea.

The critical method suggested by realism begins by detaching the literary work being studied from its context in literature. After that, the work may be discussed in relation to its historical, social, biographical, and other nonliterary affinities. Such a method, inadequate as it is, is often rationalized as a proper emphasis on the "uniqueness" of the work. At this point, perhaps, we can see the weak spot in the traditional form-content distinction: what is called content is the structure of the particular or individual work. With romance it is much harder to avoid the feeling of convention, that the story is one of a family of similar stories. Hence in the criticism of romance we are led very quickly from what the individual work says to what the entire convention it belongs to is saying through the work. This way of putting it may be critically somewhat illiterate, but, like other illiterate statements, it may have its own simple eloquence. The reading of an individual romance, say a detective story or a Western, may be in itself a trivial enough imaginative experience. But a study of the whole convention of Westerns or detective stories would tell us a good deal about the shape of stories as a whole, and that, in its turn, would begin to give us some glimpse of still larger verbal structures, eventually of the mythological universe itself.

The mythological universe has two aspects. In one aspect it is the verbal part of man's own creation, what I call a secular scripture; there is no difficulty about that aspect. The other is, traditionally, a revelation given to man by God or other powers beyond himself. These two aspects take us back to Wallace Stevens' imagination and reality. Reality, we remember, is otherness, the sense of something not ourselves. We naturally think of the other as nature, or man's actual environment, and in the divided world of work and ego-control it is nature. But for the imagination it is rather some kind of force or power or will that is not ourselves, an otherness of spirit. Not all of us will be satisfied with calling the central part of our mythological inheritance a revelation from God, and, though each chapter in this book closes on much the same cadence, I cannot claim to have found a more acceptable formulation. It is quite true that if there is no sense that the mythological universe is a human creation, man can never get free of servile anxieties and superstitions, never surpass himself, in Nietzsche's phrase. But if there is no sense that it is also something uncreated, something coming from elsewhere, man remains a Narcissus staring at his own reflection, equally unable to surpass himself. Somehow or other, the created scripture and the revealed scripture, or whatever we call the latter, have to keep fighting each other like Jacob and the angel, and it is through the maintaining of this struggle, the suspension of belief between the spiritually real and the humanly imaginative, that our own mental evolution grows. Meanwhile we have one principle to go on with. The improbable, desiring, erotic, and violent world of romance reminds us that we are not awake when we have abolished the dream world: we are awake only when we have absorbed it again.

3

Our Lady of Pain: Heroes and Heroines of Romance

3

IN THE ETHICAL scheme of Dante's *Inferno*, there are two modes of sin, *forza* and *froda*, violence and fraud, and every sin is committed under one or other of these aspects. Ethically, *froda* ranks lower than *forza*, because its use of disguise and concealment makes it more difficult to recognize as vice. Hence there is a greater imaginative appeal in *forza*. *Forza* and *froda* also organize the demonic part of *Paradise Lost*. They are contrasted in the speeches of Moloch and Belial respectively in Book Two, where Moloch wants an all-out assault on heaven and Belial suggests concealment. The Limbo of Vanities, or Paradise of Fools, in Book Three consists of souls who have tried to take the kingdom of heaven either by violence, through suicide, or by fraud, through hypocrisy.

For the study of literature we need a principle which is that of Mandeville's *Fable of the Bees* in reverse: public vices become private benefits. *Forza* and *froda* being the two essential elements of sin, it follows that they must be the two cardinal virtues of human life as such. Machiavelli personified them as the lion and the fox, the force and cunning which together make up the strong prince. So it is not surprising that European literature should begin with the celebration of these two mighty powers of humanity, of *forza* in the *Iliad*, the story of the wrath (*menis*) of Achilles, of *froda* in the *Odyssey*, the story of the guile (*dolos*) of Ulysses.

When violence and fraud enter literature, they help to create the forms of tragedy and comedy respectively. The tragic hero is normally a person capable of being an agent and not merely a victim of violence, but tragedy is mainly a form in which an actual or potential agent of violence becomes a victim of it. As *forza* is open violence, tragedy seldom conceals anything essential from audience or reader. We know who murdered Duncan and Hamlet senior; we know what Iago's honesty amounts to; we know that Goneril and Regan are evil before they quite realize it themselves. And when we ask what it is that brings the tragic hero to grief, we find that it is often a deficiency in dealing with fraud. Othello is violent, but cannot see through the fraud of Iago; Macbeth is violent and attempts fraud, but his conscience makes the fraud very unconvincing; in Hamlet, violence and guile are spasmodic, as he plunges into each in turn. To have murdered Claudius in cold blood with his back turned would have been the act of Machiavelli's strong prince, violence and cunning united in perfect heroic integrity. Such a resolution to the play would still have been tragic, but tragic with a strong reassuring major chord of deliverance from a nightmare, such as we have at the end of *Macbeth*.

Peacock's well-known essay on the four ages of poetry says that poetry begins in the flattery of barbarian rulers, the poets being hired to eulogize their robberies and cruelties. Certainly one can find evidence that this has been an important social function of poets. In the Scandinavian Saga of Harold Hardradi (the name means "hard ruler," or ruthless), a poet is quoted who bursts into song like this:

No poet can with justice
Describe the royal vengeance
That left the Uplands farmsteads
Derelict and empty.
In eighteen months, King Harold
Earned himself renown;
His acts will be remembered
Until the end of time.

The corresponding pattern in romance is the story of the hero who goes through a series of adventures and combats in which he always wins. Marlowe's Tamburlaine, for instance, appears to have been uniformly successful up to the moment of his death. But even death is a defeat of sorts, hence there is an inner dialectic in the eulogy of power which tends to make all heroes of action ultimately tragic heroes. Often a hero seems to be trying to achieve some kind of liberation for himself through his physical strength. Such liberation may be symbolized by invulnerability, as in the stories of Achilles, Samson, Hercules, and Grettir the Strong. But sooner or later some chink in the armor opens up and the hero is destroyed.

The success of the hero derives from a current of energy which is partly from him and partly outside him. It depends partly on the merit of his courage, partly on certain things given him: unusual strength, noble blood, or a destiny prophesied by an oracle. The most basic term for this current of energy is luck (Icelandic *gaefa*). Luck is highly infectious: the lucky man can always form a *comitatus* or group of devoted followers around him. Once he has lost his luck, he finds that bad luck is equally infectious: the unlucky man must be avoided like the plague, because in a sense he is the plague. When Ulysses in Homer returns to

Aeolus to explain that through no fault of his own he has run into misfortune, Aeolus tells him to clear out, that an unlucky man is hated by the gods, and he will have nothing more to do with him.

A hero may lose his luck in various ways: sometimes through a self-destructive quality in himself, expressed by such words as "fey" or "hybris," sometimes through the kind of accident that is clearly not quite an accident, such as the death of Achilles through a wound in his vulnerable heel. Most commonly, however, the hero is brought down by some form of *froda*, usually some magical or other power which may be physically weak but is strong in other areas that the hero cannot control. Such a power is often wielded, or symbolized, by a treacherous woman. Shakespeare's Mark Antony, caught in the toils of Cleopatra, finds that he has lost his luck even in the simplest sense of not being able to win games of chance with Caesar.

The comic story is more particularly the story of guile and craft, the triumph of *froda*. Its themes often feature disguise and concealment of identity, both from other characters and from the audience, and its plot normally moves toward an end acceptable to the audience but unlikely under the conditions of the action, so that some surprising or unexpected event is needed to resolve the conclusion. Its literary model is the *Odyssey*. It is Ulysses who devises the stratagems of the Trojan horse and the escape from Polyphemus, and who according to Lucian is the model of literary liars. Such qualities arouse the unstinted admiration of the goddess Athene, who feels a deep kinship with a mortal who, despite his limited human area of activity, is so superbly crooked. He is, she says, very like her:

Cunning must he be and knavish, who would go beyond thee in all manner of guile, aye, though it were a god that met thee. Bold man, crafty in counsel, insatiate in deceit, not even in thine own land, it seems, wast thou to cease from guile and deceitful tales, which thou lovest from the bottom of thine heart. But come, let us no longer talk of this, being both well versed in craft, since thou art far the best of all men in counsel and in speech, and I among all the gods am famed for wisdom and craft.

There are several things to notice in this speech. One is that there are obviously trickster gods: one thinks, among many examples, of the infant Hermes in the Homeric Hymn, who grew up to be the patron of thieves. It is clear that the goddess of wisdom (*metis*) is also a goddess of guile (*kerdosyne*). Athene, Ulysses, and probably Homer as well, have no notion of disinterested or contemplative wisdom: wisdom for them means practical sense, and includes, on the human plane, the ability to get out of a tight spot. Then again, Athene is a female deity. In Homeric conditions of life—that is, the conditions assumed in the literary conventions adopted by the Homeric poems—the physical weakness of woman makes craft and guile her chief weapons, and when women in the heroic code are violent, like Clytemnestra or Medea, they normally operate by magic or through male proxies.

Ulysses himself, of course, is a genuine hero, on the titanic scale of all Homer's warriors. It is he alone who can string the great bow, and, except in the cave of Polyphemus, he turns to craft, as Athene implies, not out of weakness, but out of sheer exuberance. Considering this, there seems to be something very curious about the second half of the poem. The situation looks like the ancient story type in which a heroine is besieged by a number of suitors, pro-

Like Tobit

except that the ordeal isn't voluntary on the part of the woman

poses some ordeal to them, and chooses the one who passes the ordeal, while the others lose their lives. Examples of the theme range from the Greek Atalanta to the eighteenth-century story of Turandot; Grimm is full of it, and we also found it at the beginning of the Apollonius romance. In the *Odyssey* Penelope is not strong enough to set up the traditional situation in which her suitors can get eliminated by ordeals or tests: her weakness forces her to resort to fraud, in the form of weaving and unweaving her web as a device for stalling them off. But one wonders whether Homer is not giving us a rationalized version of a matriarchal story which was Penelope-centered and not Ulysses-centered, in which Penelope's right to choose her suitor was unconditioned by any previous commitment. This would bring the *Odyssey* into line with Robert Graves' "white goddess" type of story. Samuel Butler, reflecting a more Victorian attitude, suggests that Penelope, or some votary of hers, wrote the *Odyssey* herself, taking care to whitewash her own morality in the process.

A Penelope-centered *Odyssey* would be a more "primitive" version of Homer's story, but, remembering the account we gave earlier of the word primitive, a more primitive version of Homer is not necessarily one that existed before Homer, but one that comes into existence whenever literature adopts "primitive" conventions, which it does every so often throughout its history. Such primitive periods usually begin with what is called "decadence," a moralized term of which the structural meaning is an exhaustion of possibilities in a previous development. In Greek heroic literature, this point is first reached with the tragic structure of Euripides.

Women in Greek tragedy are more frequently victims than agents of a tragic situation, and hence they intensify the tragic mood rather than the tragic action. In such a play as *The Trojan Women* the tragic mood is so strong that it drives us into a moral resistance to tragedy, into a feeling that the whole Trojan enterprise was wrong or silly rather than heroic, or even inevitable. Euripides, by using his women in this way, increases the tragic emotion, which may be why Aristotle calls him the most tragic of poets, and at the same time weakens the ethos that put tragedy into the center of Greek literature. His contemporary Aristophanes applies a parallel principle to comedy: in a society still male-dominated, female initiative is an effective comic device, as in the sexual strike organized by Lysistrata. Aristophanes also frequently puts Euripides into his plays, at least once (in *Thesmophoriazusae*) in a way which significantly relates him to his female characters.

Euripides and Aristophanes were succeeded by the writers of New Comedy. The audience for this was closer to what we should call a petit-bourgeois audience, one that wanted some reflection in its plays of its own primarily mercantile ethos. Hence New Comedy developed a form which regularly portrays the victory of the weak over the strong, of the young over the old, of women over their lords, of slaves over masters. The young man wants his girl, and normally gets her, with the aid of a tricky slave. The slave may confront a situation in which failure could mean crucifixion, but he invariably triumphs. New Comedy thus features a plot in which the driving force is what we have been calling fraud. It may take the form of disguise or deliberate deception, of the concealment of the identity of the main characters from other characters and the audience, of overhearing conversations, of telling cock-and-bull stories with hypocritically simulated emotions. Whatever it is, it wins. What loses is *forza* or violence: the *senex* may rave in fury and utter the most frightful threats, backed with the power to carry them out, but he is finally rendered helpless.

After New Comedy we come to the romances, of which

the most elaborate and best written is the *Ethiopica* of Heliodorus, and the simplest and most familiar the *Pastoralia,* or *Daphnis and Chloe,* of Longus. In Heliodorus particularly we can see how the story is constructed around the heroine Chariclea, not the hero Theagenes, and how everything depends on a seventeen-year-old girl's craft and wiliness. Theagenes is descended from Achilles, and every so often he puts on some kind of heroic stunt, like capturing a runaway bull. But the author has to remind himself that he has a hero, whereas Chariclea never long disappears from the center of the action. We first see them with Chariclea bending tenderly over her wounded lover: we later discover that there has been a battle, that Theagenes has fought gallantly, but that Chariclea, sniping from a concealed position, has picked off most of the enemy with bow and arrow.

In *Daphnis and Chloe* exposed infants are discovered and adopted by rustics, and the children grow up among the lambs and kids—one almost wonders whether this kind of pastoral imagery is the origin of our word "kids." They get sexually interested in each other, mainly as a result of taking baths together, but nothing comes of it, and the illustrations supplied by the animals do not seem helpful. Daphnis is then taken firmly in hand by a married woman: she adds, however, a footnote on the difference between married women and virgins, and the thought of making his Chloe bleed throws Daphnis into such a panic that his lovemaking promptly goes back to square one. Eventually the plot thins, the secret of the two births is cleared up, Daphnis and Chloe are wedded, and, in the last sentence of the story, bedded.

It looks as though there were some structural principle in this type of story which makes it natural to postpone the first sexual act of the heroine, at least, until after the birth mystery in the plot has been solved. Certainly this is the view of Heliodorus' Chariclea. Throughout the ten books of her adventures, which are spent mainly with pirates, soldiers, and other nonvirginal types, Chariclea pursues, unremittingly, three objectives. The first is to marry Theagenes; the second is to solve the mystery of her origin and find out who she is; the third is to defend her virginity from everyone, including Theagenes, until after that mystery is dispelled. Or, as she says:

I may be sure by Theagenes' oath, that he shall not fleshly have to do with me, until I have recovered my country, and parents, or if the gods be not content herewith, at least until I by mine own free will be content he shall marry me. Otherwise never.

One can, of course, understand an emphasis on virginity in romance on social grounds. In the social conditions assumed, virginity is to a woman what honor is to a man, the symbol of the fact that she is not a slave. Behind all the "fate worse than death" situations that romance delights in, there runs the sense that a woman deprived of her virginity, by any means except a marriage she has at least consented to, is, to put it vulgarly, in an impossible bargaining position. But the social reasons for the emphasis on virginity, however obvious, are still not enough for understanding the structure of romance.

We notice that, just as a man may defend his honor without necessarily having any virtue except the courage to do so, so Chariclea's dedication to virginity is not part of a general commitment to moral integrity. It certainly does not imply that she is also truthful or straightforward; in fact a more devious little twister would be hard to find among heroines of romance. Whenever she is approached by a man unsympathetic to her virginal ambitions, which includes practically every man she meets in anything like her own age group, she adopts some ruse which enables her to avoid the threat without open resistance. When she comes upon a sorceress animating the corpse of a dead son on a battlefield, her protector and guardian tells her that this is an unlawful rite and gets her away, but not without a strong desire on her part to turn the situation to her own advantage. At the end of the story she remarks resignedly, in a soliloquy, that as nobody believes her anyway she should perhaps try telling the truth, but she is relieved of this burden by the arrival of the recognition scene.

Yet of course her policy of lying is advantageous to the author, because it causes some of the complications that lengthen his book. This is part of what I mean by saying that craft or fraud is the animating spirit of the comic form. When hero and heroine go through one adventure after another, always threatened with disaster and yet somehow escaping, the plot acquires a wriggling, serpentine quality reminding one of the labyrinthine caves which so often occur in the setting. It also reflects the kind of delaying tactics that the heroine engages in. Marvell writes a poem to a "coy" mistress, fending her lover off to the end of time, in which he speaks of her "quaint honour." The etymology of the words coy and quaint, from *quietus* and *cognitus* respectively, and implying something both concealed and knowledgeable, is significant. We may compare the etymology of a word often attached to females in our day, the word "cute."

Secrecy, including disguise, is a necessary part of the heroine's tactics, partly because she is so often in a position where the hero must be convinced that he is acting on his own initiative. In Terence's *Andria*, the action, as is usual in Roman comedy, takes place on the street, much of it outside the heroine's house. A group of males, a young man, his friend, his slave, his father, the friend's father, a stranger bearing the *cognitio*, run around busily, plotting, scheming, lying, eavesdropping, threatening, resolving, revealing, misunderstanding, and exclaiming. Inside, the heroine, who has no speaking part in the action, beyond one lugubrious wail offstage as her labor pains come on, is giving birth to the hero's son. If we turn the action inside out, so to speak, we find ourselves in this silent and darkened room, where the heroine is quietly gathering all the threads of the action into her hands. Somehow or other she is going to establish her pedigree, marry the hero, present him with a male heir, and force her prospective father-in-law to like the situation. This side of the action is never alluded to, unless the fact that the play is named after her constitutes such an allusion. The heroine works under cover, in disguise or in secret until it is time for her identity to be recognized.

In such New Comedy plots as that of *Andria*, where the action is suddenly reversed near the end, the reversal includes a discovery about the heroine's identity, normally one which makes her a free citizen instead of a prostitute or slave, by virtue of having been stolen by pirates in infancy or what not. This device of the heroine's being both slave and free has had an amazing vitality in romantic comedy, and persists almost unchanged at least through the eighteenth century, despite the altered social conditions. In Goldsmith's *She Stoops to Conquer* the heroine disguises herself as a maid to attract the attention of an immature hero, who can see serving maids, through the haze of class prejudice, as things to be fondled and flirted with, but cannot endure the sight of a woman on his own social level. The word "conquer" in the title perhaps suggests that he will continue to be something of an emotionally dependent inferior. The opposite situation appears in Richardson's *Pamela*, where the heroine first appears as a symbol of class aggression to the hero, that is, essentially, as a slave. She refuses to play this role, and resists until the hero is compelled to marry her on her own terms. *Pamela* is subtitled "Virtue Rewarded," but "Virginity Rewarded" would give a clearer idea of the structure. Here again virginity is female honor, the symbol of the heroine's sturdy middle-class independence. In both stories the heroine's life is lived on two social levels: we have already seen why this movement of the action from one level to another is so important in romantic narrative.

The Fanny Price of Jane Austen's *Mansfield Park* also has a double social identity, being a poor relation brought up in a wealthy home. She has, in typical heroine fashion, decided on her cousin, Edmund Bertram, but she has to cope with a most flattering proposal favored by everybody except her. Fanny appears to be a humble, acquiescent, even passive young woman, but while she blushes and weeps and agonizes and is overwhelmed with confusion, she is also directed by a steely inflexible will that is determined to have Edmund or nobody. As her guardian Sir Thomas Bertram says, with the exasperation of a man who discovers that his society is less male-dominated than he had been assuming: "But you have now shewn me that you can be wilful and perverse, that you can and will decide for yourself."

Fanny clearly has Jane Austen's own sympathy, as is obvious from the way that the story is worked out. At the same time it is also clear that the kind of authority Sir Thomas represents seems to Jane Austen a right and natural authority. It is not that Jane Austen is a woman novelist expressing a woman's resistance to social conditions governing the place of women in her time. She accepts those conditions, on the whole: it is the romantic convention she is using that expresses the resistance. This principle that an element of social protest is inherent in romance is one that we can only suggest now, and will return to later. Meanwhile we may note that in *Emma* the hero has a moral ascendancy over the heroine which is fully justified by his greater maturity and common sense. Yet what actually happens at the end of the book is that the heroine takes on a matriarchal role, and compels him to move from his house into hers, in order not to disturb her father's dedication to inertia.

Most of Shakespeare's comedies are dominated by a similar type of heroine, and Shakespeare drew many of his comic plots from contemporary romances which are more uninhibited than he is in their treatment of the conventions. Thus in Barnabe Riche's story *Apolonius and Silla*, a source of *Twelfth Night*, the heroine, finding that the lover she has determined on has left the country without paying any attention to her, gets into a ship in pursuit of him. The captain goes into his rape-or-else routine almost before he has pulled up his anchor; the heroine prays to whatever god looks after heroines in these situations; a storm smashes the ship, and she floats to shore on the captain's chest, which is full of money and clothes, thereby enabling her both to dress up as a boy and to support herself while running her chosen man to earth. Shakespeare's heroines are usually in more complex situations, and have to be more ingenious. Rosalind in *As You Like It* keeps inventing fictions up to the very end of the action. Her remark at the end of the fourth act might be a motto for such heroines: "I shall devise something: but, I pray you, commend my counterfeiting to him." Helena in *All's Well* is also a deviser and a counterfeiter: the opposite situation occurs in *Measure for Measure*, where the heroine is determined

on virginity, with the dramatic action, much of it under-
taken by herself, pulling her in the opposite direction.
These plays turn on the folktale device of the bed trick, a
drastic but effective way of getting the hero into his predestined bed.

In such romances the heroine's role is primarily concerned with her relation to the man whom she, or her creator, is determined she shall marry, come hell or high
water, both of which do come with remarkable frequency
in romance. In this role she is a potential bride, and if her
virginity is emphasized, it is so merely as part of the exten-
sion of the story. This principle may not apply primarily
to the heroine at all. My one-volume edition of *Tom Jones*
runs to 886 pages, and it is not until page 883 that we
finally read about "that happy hour which had surren-
dered the charming Sophia to the eager arms of her enrap-
tured Jones." Sophia has doubtless remained virginal up to
that point, but Jones certainly has not; yet it is he who
must be satisfied that his series of amorous conquests has
not included his own mother before he can achieve a properly quiet consummation for his reader.

It may be thought that I am considerably laboring what
is after all a fairly rudimentary principle of dramatic structure in various fields, the principle that the G-string comes
off last. But it is precisely the elementary facts of structure
that we are so inclined to overlook, and the social facts
that we are inclined to exaggerate. One of the social facts is
that in a male-dominated society a man often assumes that
he ought to get a virgin at marriage, otherwise he may feel
that he has acquired a secondhand possession. Yet it seems
clear that romance, even when it comes to terms with this
notion, is talking about something else in its emphasis on
virginity.

It reflects another social fact of male-oriented conventions that the heroine of romance is supposed to carry out her tactics in low profile, that is, behave with due modesty. It follows that the conventions may look more realistic and iconoclastic if she is given a more active role. *All's Well That Ends Well* has the reputation of being more realistic than some of Shakespeare's other plays, mainly because the heroine makes it so clear from the beginning what she wants. This conventional iconoclasm is the central principle of many of the comedies of Bernard Shaw, where a busy, bustling, managing heroine so often dominates the stage. She is usually the spokesman of revolutionary common sense, with the males around her spouting various forms of reactionary ideology. In *Too True To Be Good* the action, or what passes for action, ends with a haunting and eloquent speech by a character first introduced as a burglar. Shaw, however, notes that the audience is left hanging on the ideological rhetoric of a male speaker, and adds a note to the printed text explaining that such talk is all very well, but of course what is really important is what the heroine does. "His own favorite is the woman of action," he says of himself. The note sounds a trifle senile in its context, and yet, of course, it is true that the heroine's activity is the mainspring not only of this comedy (the action of which is really her own wish-fulfillment dream), but of a great deal of comedy in general. The normal motive for the Shavian heroine is given by the heroine of the same play, when she says: "I have the instincts of a good housekeeper: I want to clean up this filthy world and keep it clean." Shaw's heroines have only an incidental interest in marriage, often none at all: their role is primarily maternal, and they are psychologically virgin mothers. This situation comes into its sharpest focus in *Saint Joan*, which raises issues that take us into another area.

There are two major structural principles in fiction: one

is the polarization of ideal and abhorrent worlds, which we have seen is central to romance; the other is the cycle of nature, in which the solar and seasonal cycles are associated in imagery with the cycle of human life. The heroine who becomes a bride, and eventually, one assumes, a mother, on the last page of a romance, has accommodated herself to the cyclical movement: by her marriage, or whatever it is, she completes the cycle and passes out of the story. We are usually given to understand that a happy and well-adjusted sexual life does not concern us as readers. The heroine's virginity, on the other hand, is associated with the stresses and complications she has to go through before marriage, and which constitute the story proper. She may of course be married, as she is in the *Odyssey* or in Chaucer's *Franklin's Tale,* but there her loyalty to her husband puts her symbolically in the same situation. Virginity or married loyalty is her normal state during the endurance, suffering, suspense, and terror which precede her real life after the story. The two poles of her career in the story, therefore, are her eventual triumph, which usually includes both marriage and the recovery of her identity, and, opposite, the point of her lowest fortunes, when she is often a sacrificial victim or near victim, threatened with rape or death, if not both.

At the end of Heliodorus' story, Chariclea discovers that she is the daughter of the Queen of Ethiopia, although she is white and the Ethiopians are black. The explanation is that when she was conceived her mother had her eyes fixed on a picture of Andromeda during the orgasm, and the result of this was a white baby. The queen suspects that her fellow Ethiopians may find this explanation less plausible than the author apparently does, and smuggles the infant out of the country. Chariclea arrives back in Ethiopia as a captive taken in war, to be sacrificed according to custom. The role played by Andromeda's picture in her conception indicates that she herself, in one aspect, is an Andromeda figure, a heroine exposed for a sacrifice which she narrowly avoids. The human sacrifice, usually of a virginal female, is astonishingly persistent as the crucial episode of romance: we meet it in the sixth book of *The Faerie Queene*, and it is still going strong in the late prose romances of William Morris.

As a rule the heroine avoids this fate, and so has the role of a snatched-away sacrificial victim. The virgin as sacrificial victim takes us back to Jephthah's daughter in the Bible and to Iphigeneia in Euripides, and Euripides gives us the snatched-away version of it. Iphigeneia is rescued by Artemis and taken off to Tauris on the Black Sea, where she becomes, not unnaturally, the priestess of a cult of human sacrifice. Her father Agamemnon is portrayed by Euripides as a rather weak figure, and the theme of a heroine exposed to a sacrificial situation by a foolish or inattentive father has run all through fiction. Sheridan LeFanu's *Uncle Silas* has a heroine whose father, a somewhat dithery Swedenborgian, is obsessed by the notion that his brother Silas, who is a thoroughly bad lot, has been gravely misunderstood, and sends his daughter to Silas' house, where she very nearly gets murdered. In Meredith's *The Egoist* the heroine is pushed toward marriage with the "egoist" anti-hero, largely through her father's utter inability to understand anything that goes on outside the range of his own comfort. This novel is technically more displaced than *Uncle Silas*, but the imagery linking the heroine to the Iphigeneia situation is more explicit. The same theme appears in Shakespeare. Portia, undergoing the ordeal of the caskets, which has been arranged by her father for unstated reasons, and in danger of being married to two undesirable suitors, says "I stand here for sacrifice," with a reference to Hesione, another female sacrificial victim who was rescued by Hercules.

Sometimes, of course, the heroine has to go through with her sacrificial role. Jephthah's daughter does, and so do a number of others down to the heroine of the eighteenth-century French romance *Paul et Virginie*. The somewhat inevitably named Virginie goes back from an idyllic island in the Indian Ocean to civilization and petticoats, then sets out again for the island and arrives within sight of it as a result of the usual shipwreck. Urged to remove her petticoats and save herself from drowning, she elects to drown with one hand on her heart and the other on her clothes: a triumph of propriety over self-preservation somewhat unusual even in this quixotic genre. Yet it is in keeping with the conventions of romance, where even a purely symbolic rape may still be, or represent, a fate worse than death.

Shaw's *Saint Joan* is again a play about the sacrifice of a virgin. Joan is hated even by those she redeems from English tyranny, not because of her skill and courage, but because she cannot help telling the brusque truths of common sense to those who must live on lies and illusions. The play ends with an epilogue showing that if Joan returned to earth in Shaw's own time she would get much the same rejection, if less brutal treatment. It may be significant that in the main action of the play Shaw portrays her as belonging, not so much to a higher world as to a future one, a world of nationalism and Protestantism. This seems to me a pedantic and misleading treatment of her, and one that indicates a final unconscious irony in the play. Shaw himself, apparently, cannot accommodate Joan or Joan's "voices" into his twentieth-century world without a process of rationalization which, in a very real sense, explains her away. This is an example of how a writer whose actual structures are close to romance can be misled by what he thinks of as realism.

The virgin who marries at the end of the story, we saw, represents the structural principle of the cycle and of accommodation to it. The virgin who is sacrificed, or escapes sacrifice and remains a virgin, similarly symbolizes the other principle, the separation or polarizing of the action into two worlds, one desirable and the other detestable. This is one reason why we often get two heroines in romantic literature, one associated with virginity and the other with love and marriage. Thus Spenser, in the third book of *The Faerie Queene*, portrays the virtue of chastity through Belphoebe, a Diana figure vowed to virginity, and also through Britomart, who is equally virginal for the action of the poem, but who is in love and fully intends to marry. Belphoebe is more explicitly associated with Queen Elizabeth, because Elizabeth was a virgin queen, but as long as there was a possibility of her changing her status the poet had to keep Britomart in reserve. It is obvious that in a romance, which is almost by definition a love story, there is a technical difficulty of what one does with a permanently virginal figure, even if not immobilized by allegorical association with a queen. Belphoebe stays in her wood hunting stags: it is Britomart who goes out on adventures disguised as a man, like Shakespeare's heroines.

Milton's *L'Allegro* and *Il Penseroso*, which contain almost everything essential to an understanding of romance, also give us a clue to the significance of these two heroine figures. In *Il Penseroso* the poet's mistress is a personified "Melancholy," who is a nun, a vestal virgin rather than a Christian nun. (To the extent that she could be a Christian nun she would represent a purely aesthetic approach to Christianity, like the cloisters, stained glass windows, organ music, and hermitage of the closing lines.) Such a melancholy mistress forms a contrast to the "heart-easing Mirth" of *L'Allegro*, who is presumably more liberal, though the poet is cautious about defining the extent of her favors. However, it seems clear that Mirth represents the normal idyllic conclusion, and Melancholy a withdrawal from it into solitude: this contrast of cadences in romance will be a recurrent theme from here on. We begin to see the possibility of a further development of the theme of virginity, one which represents a lifelong sublimation expressing itself as a commitment, or spiritual marriage, to something impersonal, such as religious devotion or a political cause. Such a figure would represent, or at least point to, a world above that of the main action of the story.

In Scott's *Waverley* there are two heroines, Rose Bradwardine and Flora MacIvor. Waverley is more attracted to Flora at first, but she refuses him outright. She is wholly committed to the Jacobite cause, and she realizes that Waverley has only blundered into his Jacobitism. When the cause collapses, she retires to a convent on the Continent. Meanwhile the hero goes through various adventures about which there is a good deal of mystery, with a female shape fluttering in and out of his quarters. Eventually this proves to be Rose Bradwardine, arranging the plot in typical heroine fashion, until the hero is ready to know which woman he ought to be marrying. Flora is a quixotic figure like Waverley himself, though a considerably more impressive one, and to some extent she does reflect the mores of Scott's society, in which, as a rule, a successful female career consists of a good marriage and retirement to a convent is a sign of maladjustment. Nevertheless, Flora is much the more memorable of the two heroines: in fact, she and her brother, with his tragic fate, upstage the whole cast.

In Scott's later novel *The Pirate* we have two sisters, Minna and Brenda Troil, who are explicitly contrasted along Miltonic lines as grave and gay, penseroso and allegro types. The melancholy sister Minna is a romantic devoted to a cause of a type that a Canadian reader would call separatism. When a pirate named Cleveland appears in the story she feels strongly attracted to him because she regards pirates as symbols of the kind of romantic rebelliousness she favors. The heroines are then abducted: Cleveland, however, makes something of a habit of forgoing his sexual demands, having previously saved the honor of two Spanish ladies in earlier forays. As the Spanish ladies were really "persons of quality," his record of abstinence saves him from being hanged. However, there is enough heavy breathing to convince Minna that she has been wrong about pirates, and the penalty for her mistake in judgment is perpetual virginity.

In *Ivanhoe* there are again two heroines, the Saxon Rowena and the Jewish Rebecca. Rowena is determined to marry the man of her choice, but has otherwise few distinguishing characteristics except her blonde hair. Rebecca is menaced in the usual style by a Norman noble, Brian de Bois-Guilbert, and she also nearly becomes a sacrificial victim, because Brian's superior in the Templar order is an obsessed bigot who wants to convict her of sorcery. With the figure of Rebecca, the innocent victim of a venomous bigotry who remains steadfast in her faith, we begin to see that romance, in its stress on the theme of virginity, may be talking about something more than the condition of the hymen membrane.

At the lowest point of such a heroine's career, when her innocence and gentleness are most strongly contrasted with the malignancy of the powers arrayed against her, she gives the impression of someone living in a world below the one that she ought to be living in. Hence she is, mythically, in the position of a goddess in a lower world. When we come to this mythical core of a common, even a hackneyed situation, we come back to the problem I mentioned before, of having to distinguish what the individual story is saying from what the convention the story belongs to is saying through the story.

In another Greek romance by Achilles Tatius, *Cleitophon and Leucippe*, which is, by and large, a rather silly story, the heroine is separated from her lover, is kidnapped and reduced to slavery, is threatened with torture and lashes; yet she still defies her tormentors and talks about the freedom of her soul. We can distinguish between the preposterous and contrived melodrama of this particular romance, and the convention expressed by it, where some kind of genuine human dignity does come through. Deep within the stock convention of virgin-baiting is a vision of human integrity imprisoned in a world it is in but not of, often forced by weakness into all kinds of ruses and stratagems, yet always managing to avoid the one fate which really is worse than death, the annihilation of one's identity. In Achilles Tatius we are a very long way, in power and splendor, from anything like "I am Duchess of Malfi still." But we are in the same imaginative area for all that. If we want an image, or objective correlative, for this kind of integrity, there is an exquisite one in Sidney's *Arcadia*, where the heroine wears a diamond set in a black horn, with the motto attached "yet still myself." What is symbolized as a virgin is actually a human conviction, however expressed, that there is something at the core of one's infinitely fragile being which is not only immortal but has discovered the secret of invulnerability that eludes the tragic hero.

The simplest way out of the sacrificial situation, for the storyteller, is the Proserpine solution. When Proserpine is seized by a demon lover and carried off into a world of death, she touches the food of death, to the extent of eating some pomegranate seeds. Here the communion image of food replaces the sexual one: eating the seeds is a sacrificial act in which what is sacrificed is symbolically her virginity. As a result she has to spend half of each year in the lower world and half above, revolving with the cycle of nature. She is the archetype of all romantic virgins who marry and live "happily" ever after. It is possible that some of these heroines, if their happy post-narrative lives were more fully investigated, would be found, like Proserpine, to be spending at least half their time in hell. But occasionally we realize that this is not the whole area of romance, and that some heroines may symbolize not only a descent from a higher world but a permanent return to it.

We notice that Rebecca in *Ivanhoe* has near-miraculous powers of healing: this theme often recurs in romance, attached mainly to virtuous females like the Helena of *All's Well*, and sometimes dependent on the physical preservation of virginity. The bigotry in Rebecca's society is so perverted that it is precisely her life-giving powers that bring her under suspicion of sorcery. This suggests that the beleaguered virgin may be more than simply a representative of human integrity: she may also exert a certain redemptive quality by her innocence and goodness, or, in other contexts, by her astuteness in management and intrigue.

At the heart of all literature is what I have called the cycle of *forza* and *froda*, where violence and guile are coiled up within each other like the yin-and-yang emblem of Oriental symbolism. Here the imaginative center is clearly in tragedy, the heroic dimension being the one that makes the greatest emotional impression on us. The heroic is associated with an often invulnerable strength, yet the heroism ends in death and the strength is not after all invulnerable. The comic side of this, the victory of guile, often takes the form of a triumph of a slave or maltreated heroine, or other figure associated with physical weakness. With the rise of the romantic ethos, heroism comes increasingly to be thought of in terms of suffering, endurance, and patience, which can coexist with such weakness, whatever other kinds of strength it may require. This is also the ethos of the Christian myth, where the heroism of Christ takes the form of enduring the Passion. Such a change in the conception of heroism largely accounts for the prominence of female figures in romance. But, as secular literature is not bound by any doctrinal inhibitions, the romantic heroine can take on a redemptive role as well, like her divine counterpart in the Christian story.

This means that the myth of romance, though closely related to the myth of Christianity, and for centuries contemporary with it, should not be thought of as derived from it. As soon as we think of redemptive female descents to a lower world we think of Euripides' Alcestis, who is pre-Christian. Alcestis prolongs her husband's life by her journey to the world of the dead to offer herself as a substitute, but she is not a redeemer herself, and has to be rescued from Death in her turn by Hercules. Her redemptive effort is achieved by sacrifice, and she is snatched from the ultimate sacrifice like Iphigeneia. She does this for a man whose general attitude to the situation is: "Well, perhaps my father should have gone instead, but certainly somebody should." As in the Christian myth, we often wonder in romance whether the people for whom the heroine's efforts are made are always worth it. Is getting the Bertram of *All's Well* worth the skill, devotion, and elaborate deceptions of Helena? Richardson's Pamela, again, contemplates with the greatest enthusiasm and affection her approaching marriage to the man who had done his level best to ruin her life.

Much older than Alcestis is the mysterious figure of Inanna, or Ishtar, who in very ancient Mesopotamian poems is shown descending into the world of the dead in full regalia, passing seven gates, at each of which some of her regalia is removed, until she arrives naked and helpless in the presence of the shades of death. Why she descends we do not know, and certainly the scene makes far more of an impact without a motive. But questions of substitutes demanded by the powers of death seem to be involved, as they are in the descent of Christ also. Keeping in mind the Christian parallel, it is as though there were two aspects to the symbolism of the sacrificial victim, one in which she is a hostage for death, and so exposed to death herself, and another in which she is what has come instead of death. In the latter aspect she is, potentially, the conqueror of death and the redeemer of its captives. One of the most fundamental of human realizations is that passing from death to rebirth is impossible for the same individual; hence the theme of substitution for death runs all through literature, religion, and ritual. Redemption is one form of substitution, though one more satisfying to theology than to romance.

In any case there are escapes and ascents as well as descents, both for the heroine herself and for those she helps. We have the Ariadne who guides Theseus out of the labyrinth, the Isis who restores Lucius to his human shape in Apuleius, the Lucia and Beatrice whose love and care get Dante through Purgatory, and other forms of the *ewig-weibliche* that draw us upward to our more deeply desired goals. Here again we have what looks like a counterpart to the Christian schema, and the one that underlies the great Eros myth in which the lover is raised to a higher world by his mistress.

The poet Yeats developed, or had suggested to him, a theory of history in which two contrasting types of civilization dominate the Western world in turn. Classical culture, in this view, was essentially a heroic culture, aristocratic and violent, its central myth being the story of Oedipus, who kills his father and lives in incest with his mother. It was succeeded by the Christian culture, which is democratic and altruistic, based on the myth of Christ, who appeases and reconciles his father, crowns his virginal mother, and rescues his bride the Church. The coming of each culture is symbolized by the conjunction of a bird and a woman, the bird being the manifestation of a god. Classical culture is heralded by the sexual union of Leda and the swan, Christian culture by the nonsexual union of the Dove and the Virgin. Tragedy is at the heart of Classical civilization, comedy at the heart of the Christian one. The progeny of Leda and the swan represent Eros and Ares, sexual love and war; the Virgin's son is divine love and a prince of peace. After the Christian cycle is ended, Yeats says, we shall return to a heroic and violent culture of the Classical type.

I do not think much of this as a general view of history; but the modulation I have been dealing with, the change from Greek tragedy through Euripides to New Comedy and thence to prose romance, is well symbolized by it. It is true that literature after Euripides, or at least the romantic literature which forms the bulk of it, is mainly under the sign of the Dove and the Virgin. But this applies whether the literature itself is pagan or Christian: it is still under the Dove and the Virgin when the dove is Venus' dove and the virgin Diana. Heliodorus and Achilles Tatius are said to have been Christian bishops, and Heliodorus, according to a legend transmitted by Montaigne, on being compelled to choose between his bishopric and acknowledging the authorship of his romance, made the only choice that any self-respecting author could make, and ceased to be a bishop. But whether these writers were Christian or not, the fictional devices employed are common to Christian and pagan romance.

I think that what I have been calling the *forza-froda* cycle is essentially Yeats's Leda and swan cycle. It was not destroyed by Christianity, but survived intact: we have the same tragic structures and heroic ethos in Shakespeare, and the old comic formulas are still working in Dickens. But the growth of what we have been calling sentimental romance takes us into a second imaginative universe. One pole of this is an idyllic world where human desires and ideals can find more scope, and where violence and fraud can occasionally be seen in the form of their corresponding virtues, fortitude and prudence. The other pole is a night world symbolized by human sacrifice, a world which is more an object of moral abhorrence than strictly a tragic one. The dove-and-virgin cycle is comedy-centered, it is true, but it is not simply the antithesis of its predecessor, as Yeats's scheme would have it. It is in some respects a more expanded world, and we sometimes have the feeling in a romance or comedy of moving from one world into a larger one. In speaking of Terence's *Andria* I said that the action seems to move simultaneously on two levels, one of the foreground action, the other inside the heroine's mind. When the action passes from one level to the other through the recognition scene, we have a feeling of going through some sort of gyre or vortex, to use another Yeats image, a feeling we express in the phrase we so inevitably use when summarizing a romantic plot: "it turns out that . . ."

Where tragedy arises in this dove-and-virgin type of literature, its effect is quite different from tragedy in Aeschylus or the *Iliad* or the mature period of Shakespeare. A romance is normally comic, in the sense that usually the heroine's wiles or whatever are successful and the story ends with marriage or some kind of deliverance. Tragedy or pathos comes from some obstacle or accident which frustrates this conclusion. A heroine may meet disaster through being betrayed or deserted by her lover, or, like Richardson's Clarissa, may fail to stick to the tried and true virginal tactics. Such romantic tragedies as *Romeo and Juliet* or *The Bride of Lammermoor* seem more like a comedy gone wrong: for all Romeo's talk about the stars, his tragedy is not built into the scheme of things as the tragedy of Lear is, or that of Oedipus before him.

Certainly there are close connections between the imaginative universe of romance and of Christianity: the myth of Christianity is also a divine comedy which contains a tragedy, and thinks of that tragedy as an episode within a larger comic structure. But they are not the same thing, and should not be confused. My last chapter will suggest that we may be moving into a third imaginative order, but I cannot see that this third order shows any sign whatever of simply returning to the first one. Not only Yeats, but several other writers, most of them insane, have believed in or proposed such a return, and in politics a parallel notion has produced the black cloud of illusion that we know as fascism. But in our day every genuine issue, in the arts as outside them, is connected with getting clear of all such notions of cyclical historical fatality.

In Blake's poem "Earth's Answer" a female Earth, called upon by the poet to stop turning in cycles and enter the world of eternal light, complains that she cannot do so because "Starry Jealousy does keep my den." This starry jealousy in Blake is the "Covering Cherub," the cosmic peacock whose eyes are the stars, and who keeps us bound to fate because he also keeps the Earth under the tyranny of unending space and time. The Covering Cherub is winged, like other angels, and the overtones of "covering" are sexual, the Earth being his *femme couverte*. The poem heralds an age when the cyclical conjunctions of divine birds and human women are finally broken, and the human imagination has passed beyond the empty heavens into its original earth.

4

The Bottomless Dream:
Themes of Descent

4

FROM THE BEGINNING the poetic imagination has inhabited a middle earth. Above it is the sky with whatever it reveals or conceals: below it is a mysterious place of birth and death from whence animals and plants proceed, and to which they return. There are therefore four primary narrative movements in literature. These are, first, the descent from a higher world; second, the descent to a lower world; third, the ascent from a lower world; and, fourth, the ascent to a higher world. All stories in literature are complications of, or metaphorical derivations from, these four narrative radicals.

Explicitly for the first eighteen centuries of the Christian era, and implicitly after and long before that, these patterns of ascent and descent have been spread over a mythological universe consisting of four main levels, two above our own, one below it. The highest level is heaven, the place of the presence of God: this world is strictly beyond space, but may be symbolized, as in Dante's *Paradiso*, by the spatial metaphor of heaven in the sense of the sky, the world of sun, moon, and stars. The world above the moon is traditionally thought of as the world that escaped the fall, and is consequently what is left of the order of nature as God originally made it. Level two is the

97

earthly paradise or Garden of Eden, where man lived before the fall. The associations of the word "fall" suggest that Eden is to be thought of as the highest point in the world, as it is geographically in Dante. Level three is the world of ordinary experience we now live in. Animals and plants seem to be well adjusted to this world, but man, though born in it, is not of it: his natural home is level two, where God intended him to live. Level four is the demonic world or hell, in Christianity not part of the order of nature but an autonomous growth, usually placed below ground.

All four of these levels are symbolically ambivalent, and these ambivalences are of great importance in the structure of romance. In Chaucer, for example, the disasters and tragedies wrought by the conjunctions of the stars in *The Knight's Tale* and *Troilus and Criseyde* make it clear that the heavens are for him, as for most science fiction writers today, much more a symbol of alienation than of divine presence. Chaucer is careful to explain this in Christian terms: stars would not have met in "synod unbenign," in Milton's phrase, if there had been no fall, and only pagans are completely subject to their malign influence. But the emotional ambivalence remains. As for the earthly paradise, according to Christian doctrine it was, but it cannot now be; consequently in romance the paradisal is frequently a deceitful illusion that turns out to be demonic, or a destructive vision. The fourth level, though purely demonic in Christianity, is in romance often a world where great rewards, of wisdom or wealth, may await the explorer.

The ambivalence in the third level of ordinary experience is of a different kind. This world seems to be hard to incorporate into the great Christian epics: Dante and Milton place their settings in heaven, hell and Eden, but thirteenth-century Italy, and seventeenth-century England, enter only through external allusion. In Spenser's *Faerie Queene*, which is more typical of romance, the world of experience is introduced through allegory, by means of the fact that the main setting of the poem, "faerie," a purgatorial world of moral realization like Dante's, is nevertheless one that occupies the same time and space as our world. But the level of ordinary experience is also represented in Spenser as a sexual world, symbolized by satyrs. These satyrs, though not quite human, are not quite evil either: they represent perhaps what human life would be like if human beings were as completely adjusted to the "fallen" level of nature as animals and plants are. Their lives consist, in Eliot's phrase, of birth and copulation and death; but they regard copulation as the only sensible way of putting in the time between birth and death. They remind us of the half of ordinary experience that is often, except in romance, ignored: the dreaming experience of the night, with its erotic resonance.

At present we are concerned with descent themes, and these fall into two groups: those that suggest descent from the sky or, more precisely, one of the two higher worlds, heaven and Eden, and those that suggest descent to a subterranean or submarine world beneath this one. In the latter, the normal road of descent is through dream or something strongly suggestive of a dream atmosphere. In the former, we meet first of all the familiar motifs of the birth of the quasi-divine hero, who really has two fathers, his real father, who is a god, and his assumed father, who is normally the husband of his human mother. His birth often arouses the jealousy of the assumed father; hence the common romance theme of the calumniated mother, who is sentenced to death with her infant but escapes, or is put out to sea in an empty boat or raft, or has her child ex-

posed. Shrouding and concealment are natural conse-
quences of a threatened birth, and the infant hidden by a
terrified mother or nurse occurs in the myths of Zeus and
Dionysus as well as the biblical stories of Moses and Jesus.
In later literature the theme of descent from a higher world
enters the poems that speak of birth as coming down from
a state of innocence or freedom into a "prison-house," as
Wordsworth calls it, of corruption or confusion. In Victorian romance there are many stories about delicate children, who, like Blake's Thel, find this world too much for
them and return to their place of innocence. One of the
freshest and most attractive of these is George MacDonald's *At the Back of the North Wind*, the story of an imaginative little boy who makes a friend of the north wind,
then discovers and returns to a place of serenity and peace
which is "back of" the north wind, a place explicitly identified with the Garden of Eden in Dante's *Purgatorio*.

Closely linked with stories of this type is the standard
theme of the infant exposed on a hillside and picked up by
shepherds, so common in New Comedy and Classical
romance. In the Christian myth Christ, of course, comes to
this world from above (*descendit de coelis*, as the creed
says), but the Nativity stories in the Gospels show a good
many analogues to the New Comedy themes. Christ is
actually of royal descent, acknowledged by three kings (as
they later become), yet born in obscurity, besides having
his life threatened by a usurper-king. His birth takes place
in a semi-pastoral setting, a manger flanked by an ox and
an ass, surrounded with shepherds, and watched over by
the quasi-pastoral figure of Joseph, who is really his foster
father. It is not so far from this vision of peace to *Daphnis
and Chloe*, where what there is of both action and passion
is contained by an idyllic world, a pastoral setting of sexual innocence constructed out of the imagery of various

pastoral poets, including Theocritus and Sappho. The imagery of *Daphnis and Chloe* revolves around the seasonal cycle, represented in myth by the death of Adonis. Thus Daphnis' foster father has a beautiful garden, and a spiteful rival of Daphnis gets into it and tramples down all the flowers "like a boar." The climax of the story, as noted earlier, is a sexual union which is part of a spring fertility rite. There are also hints of more sinister things like wars and attacks from pirates, though none of them come to much—*Daphnis and Chloe* is a very placid story.

But for all the innocence, the idyllic pastoral world is still a second world, a world of derived identity, with a higher world above it which enters only symbolically, in the form of the discovery of the true parentage. When the two infants were exposed on the hillside, birth tokens indicating a higher social rank were put beside them: these are produced to establish their identity at the end. The fact that they simply sit there throughout the story indicates something about the nature of suspense in this type of narrative that we shall have to return to. The father who originally exposed Daphnis says that he expected Daphnis to die, and consequently the birth tokens were really intended to be death tokens. We may compare the gifts presented to the infant Jesus by the wise men, which are also, especially myrrh, emblems of the Passion.

There are said to be customs and rituals in ancient Greece that explain the child-exposing convention; but they do not explain why Victorian writers, fifteen centuries later, should be as preoccupied with it as ever. With the archetype, at least: the actual exposure and adoption procedure is found only in stories with a strong folktale feeling about them, like *Silas Marner*. Scott and Dickens would often be helpless for plot interest without the motif of mysterious birth: in Dickens a hero's parents, like those of

Oliver Twist, may be triumphantly produced at the end of the story even though they are mere names, playing no part in the story itself. In his autobiography, Trollope notes the fact that *Doctor Thorne* sold better than some of his other novels, adding the realist's customary protest: "The plot of *Doctor Thorne* is good, and I am led therefore to suppose that a good plot,—which to my own feeling, is the most insignificant part of a tale,—is that which will most raise it or most condemn it in the public judgement." In *Doctor Thorne* the heroine is not Thorne's daughter but the daughter of somebody much wealthier, so that the obstacles to her marriage with the hero are removed. After a glance at Scott and Dickens, we may say that what *Doctor Thorne* had was not *a* good plot but *the* good plot.

Whether romance begins with a hero whose birth is, as Wordsworth says, a sleep and a forgetting, or whether it begins with a sinking from a waking world into a dream world, it is logical for it to begin its series of adventures with some kind of break in consciousness, one which often involves actual forgetfulness of the previous state. We may call this the motif of amnesia. Such a catastrophe, which is what it normally is, may be internalized as a break in memory, or externalized as a change in fortunes or social context. The change in mind may be brought about by the wrath of a god, usually at the kind of errors most apt to make gods nervous, such as boastfulness. The themes of rash promise and of fatal curiosity, as when Pandora or Psyche open boxes that they should have left shut, are closely connected, implying as they do the collapse of the rightful order in the mind and the separation of consciousness from the proper rhythm of action.

The break in consciousness may also be induced by drugs, a love potion like the ones in the Tristram and Sigurd legends, or a disease like Silas Marner's catalepsy. It may be externalized as a disaster like capture by pirates, or a wandering into the land of the fairies, involving a change so drastic as to give the sense of becoming someone else altogether. Thus Alice, pressed to recount her adventures by the Mock Turtle and Gryphon, says she can tell them her adventures of that day, "but it's no good going back to yesterday, because I was a different person then." In *The Winter's Tale* a mood of jealousy explodes without warning in Leontes' mind and takes it over, replacing his former feelings about his wife with a malignant psychosis. It is really an obliteration of memory, and in another type of story it could be the result of a curse or demonic possession. In the Indian play *Sakuntala*, the prince who is the hero is betrothed to the heroine, but as a result of a curse inflicted by an irritable hermit his memory of her is destroyed. The mystery in Wilkie Collins' *The Moonstone* is about the stealing of a diamond: the solution is that it was stolen by the hero himself as a result of an anxiety dream inspired by opium, given him without his knowledge by a malicious physician.

One of the early burlesques of Jane Austen bears the title "Henry and Eliza." Eliza is discovered under a haycock at the age of three months by Sir George and Lady Harcourt. They are delighted with the precocious infant's conversation, and take her into their home as their daughter. She remains there until the age of eighteen, when, being detected in stealing a banknote of fifty pounds, "she was turned out of doors by her inhuman Benefactors." After a page or two of adventures, Eliza resolves to go back to her foster parents to see if she can hit them up for anything more. Lady Harcourt receives her with "transports of Joy," exclaiming that Eliza is not their adopted daughter but their real child. Pressed for an explanation, she says that she was left "breeding" by her husband when he went to America, that he had wanted a boy, and finding that she had produced a girl, she set the infant under a haycock and promptly forgot she had had her. The author shows a regrettable tendency to humor, which might have been of some disadvantage to her if she had continued with this genre; but she certainly knows what the genre is. Seldom has the role of amnesia in getting a story started been more clearly set forth.

At the beginning of a romance there is often a sharp descent in social status, from riches to poverty, from privilege to a struggle to survive, or even slavery. Families are separated and the hero may, like the hero of Scott's *Redgauntlet,* find himself falling in love with his sister. But the structural core is the individual loss or confusion or break in the continuity of identity, and this has analogies to falling asleep and entering a dream world. The latter is a world of increased erotic intensity, as is obvious from the imagery of romance alone, without reference to psychology. We are often reminded of this type of descent by the imagery of the hunt. A knight rides off into a forest in pursuit of an animal, and as he disappears the dream atmosphere closes around him. Sometimes he finds himself in a forest so dense that the sky is invisible. In this threshold symbol of entering a world of sleep all images begin to take on an erotic quality, so that the surrounding forest becomes a sexual personality.

The hunt is normally an image of the masculine erotic, a movement of pursuit and linear thrust, in which there are sexual overtones to the object being hunted. These overtones lead, in English, to many puns on "deer" and "hart." As we sink deeper into the dream, the quasi-sexual object of pursuit becomes the surrounding forest itself. There seems to be an increasing identity between the forest and a shrouding female body, of a rather sinister kind. This comes out vividly in the story of Actaeon, changed to a stag and hunted by his own hounds at the prompting of an elusive virginal forest goddess who is not to be seen naked. Behind various incest and Oedipal taboos is the suggestion that the hunter is seeking a false identity which is the same thing as his own destruction. The consummation of the hunt is the death of the animal, which for Actaeon is the turning of the pursuer into the victim. We are reminded of the song in *As You Like It:*

> What shall he have that kill'd the deer?
> His leather skin and horns to wear.

The song goes on to make the inevitable joke about cuckolds, but of course the cuckold with his horns is a displaced version of Actaeon, the victim of his own pursuit.

The image of the hunter pursuing an animal is never very far from metamorphosis, or the actual changing of the hunter into an animal. If it is true, as the structuralists tell us, that every structural system includes a set of transformations, metamorphoses are the normal transformations of the structure of myth. Every aspect of fall or descent is linked to a change in form in some way, usually by associating or identifying a human or humanized figure with something animal or vegetable. Daphne becomes a laurel and Syrinx a reed; Adam and Eve in Genesis, on losing their original preternatural gifts, become the rational animals symbolized by the "coats of skin" they receive from God. Even Daphnis and Chloe are almost assimilated to the animals they are brought up with. The story of Apuleius about a man metamorphosed into an ass includes an outward and social as well as a dreaming aspect of the motif. The ass is *par excellence* the proletarian animal, whose lot is slavery and incessant beating, with no chance to participate in noble life such as at least some horses have.

We get a fairly undisplaced version of hunting, metamorphosis, and exchanged identity motifs in a play of Carlo Gozzi, *Il Re Cervo* (the king stag). Here the king is turned into a stag by an enchantment he has brought about himself, and is hunted by his own hounds. His treacherous minister takes advantage of this to enter the king's body, thus becoming a demonic double of the king, who is forced to enter the body of a beggar. We also have a bird-catcher who seems to be identified to some degree with his birds, and is a comic and lowerclass version of the royal hunter. The bird he is particularly associated with is the parrot, a bird that has a natural connection with this world—we shall see why in a moment. A better known example of the bird-catcher figure appears in a very similar type of play, *The Magic Flute,* where his name, Papageno, again points to the parrot, and where the sinister shrouding female influence is represented by the Queen of the Night.

Changes in identity do not have to go all the way into metamorphosis: they may stop at sexual disguise, such as a heroine putting on boys' clothes or vice versa. Shakespeare, with his boy actors, prefers the former, but the reverse is also common: even Huckleberry Finn, in the middle of the latency period of boyhood, puts on female clothes twice. Change of name is a still simpler device, often used without any apparent motive in romance. The two heroes of Sidney's *Arcadia* have three names apiece, and one, disguised as an Amazon, is referred to as "she" as long as the disguise lasts.

If I dream about myself, I have two identities, myself as dreamer and myself as character in my dream. The dreamer is, so to speak, a god in relation to his dreamed self: he created him but remains in the background watching. The dreamer may be concerned for the fate of his double in the unknown world that the latter ventures into, but his power of rescue may vary. Sometimes the story is so told that the hero remains aware of what he was at the beginning. Rasselas and his sister, in Samuel Johnson's story, descending from their prison-paradise in Abyssinia to the lower world of Egypt, take a long time to realize that they are no longer considered of royal parentage in this lower world, but, Rasselas says, "my birth has given me at least one advantage over others, by enabling me to determine for myself." Few remarks in romance explain more clearly the essential point about the device of concealed original identity.

There is often a god behind the action of a romance, who expresses his will by some kind of oracle or prophecy which speaks of the ultimate outcome as predetermined. Such oracles are common in Greek romance, are still going strong in Elizabethan times, and survive in various forms later, the astrological predictions in *Guy Mannering* being an example. A god of this type is clearly a projection of the author himself, and as such he is placed outside the action. He becomes an alienation figure in Brecht's sense of the term, reminding us that the show is only a show after all. In some plays, including Gozzi's play just mentioned and *The Tempest*, the constructor of the action is a magician, who renounces his magic as a sign that the play is over. We have also a producer or stage manager at the beginning of *Sakuntala* and Goethe's *Faust*. A slightly different type of alienation figure is the jester, like the Touchstone who accompanies the two heroines of *As You Like It* into the forest. This jester type is clearly of some structural significance, as he appears also in the totally unrelated Sanskrit drama: he seems to be a kind of one-man chorus, speaking for the audience's desire to be entertained by the story.

Autolycus in *The Winter's Tale* is parallel: his out-
rageously unlikely ballads still have a curiously close
relationship to the kind of story being told in the play
itself. The fact that there is no trace of a Touchstone or
Autolycus figure in Shakespeare's main sources indicates
that drama, with its immediacy of impact, needs such a
focus in a way that narrative does not. In a written narrative the sense of derived identity is already contained, so to
speak, in the mode of presentation.

In the Christian story of Barlaam and Josaphat, which I
mentioned earlier, we are told that there are two natures in
Christ: without leaving his father's throne in heaven he
entered the virgin's womb: he suffered on the cross as a
man, but not as God. Whatever one thinks of this theologically, it gives us the myth of the redemptive quest of
Christ in the standard romance pattern of a double identity, one only being involved in the descent. On the other
hand Adam, after his fall, changes his identity, and the
later one may be said to be the shadow or dreaming counterpart of the one he had before. The Classical parallel to
the Adam story, as several Renaissance mythographers
noted, is the story of Narcissus, where we also have a real
man and a shadow. The mistress of Narcissus, Echo,
reminds us of the parrot or echo bird that we have already
met. What Narcissus really does is exchange his original
self for the reflection that he falls in love with, becoming,
as Blake says, "idolatrous to his own shadow." In Ovid's
story he simply drowns, but drowning could also be seen
as passing into a lower or submarine world. The reflecting
pool is a mirror, and disappearing into one's own mirror
image, or entering a world of reversed or reduced dimen-
sions, is a central symbol of descent. A study of mirror
worlds in romance might range from the Chinese novel
best known in the West by the title *The Dream of the Red*

Chamber to some remarkable treatments of the theme in science fiction, such as Arthur Clarke's *The City and the Stars* and Stanislaw Lem's *Solaris.* That narcissistic hero Peer Gynt also begins his adventures with a tale of jumping off a precipice on the back of a reindeer into the water, where a mirror image of the reindeer comes up to meet him.

Modulations of the mirror image bring us to the pictures, tapestries, and statues which so often turn up near the beginning of a romance to indicate the threshold of the romance world. Some of the Classical romances are presented to us as commentaries on pictures, which means that they attempt to recapture, or at least invoke, in words, that quality of naive and involving stare that pictures can appeal to more effectively. In Scott's *The Antiquary* the hero is put to bed in the antiquary's house in a "Green Chamber" said to be haunted and full of tapestries. "The subject was a hunting-piece . . . branches of the woven forest were crowded with fowls . . ." The hero has metamorphosis dreams in this chamber: "He was a bird— he was a fish—or he flew like the one, and swam like the other . . . wild and wonderful metamorphosis." There is a good deal of mystery about the hero's parentage, as usual, and eventually we discover that the motto for these tapestries was supplied by his mother. According to his biographer Mackail, this passage had a strong influence on William Morris, whose own romances are clearly linked to his other activities as a designer of textile patterns. The closest analogy to such picture-arts in contemporary popular culture is the television commercial, which presents its products as magical objects. On a more complex level, a similar technique appears in novels with a symbolic visual emblem, after which the novel is often named, as in *The Scarlet Letter* and *The Golden Bowl.* Even Jane Eyre produces a curious set of surrealistic pictures at the beginning of her involvement with Rochester.

Closely related is the use of special language, often with a large amount of the antiquated in it, which helps to enclose a romance like a glass case in a verbal museum. The invented languages of Tolkien come at the end of a long tradition which includes the synthetic Gothic of *Ivanhoe* and the yea-verily-and-forsooth lingo in which William Morris wrote his later prose romances and translations. Yet synthetic languages, however absurd they often sound, do seem to belong to romantic decorum: two very different contemporary examples are the Nigerian story of *The Palm Wine Drinkard* and Anthony Burgess' *A Clockwork Orange*. Sometimes the special language has a specifically dreamlike quality. There is a brutal sneer at Lady Gregory's "drivel" in *Ulysses*, but anyone listening to Joyce's own recording of the end of the ALP chapter may wonder if her "Kiltartan" idiom was not one of the central influences on the dream language of *Finnegans Wake*. Such phenomena are related to the general theme of "charm," the use of words for emotional purposes derived from the magical casting of a binding spell. This in turn is appropriate for a world where one progressively loses one's freedom of action, the lowest stage of which is imprisonment or paralysis or death itself.

The Narcissus theme helps to explain why the confusion of identity in romance is so often associated with the theme of twins. A knockabout comedy of Plautus about twins is the main source of Shakespeare's *Comedy of Errors*, which draws on the Apollonius romance for its conclusion. Critics usually note this resignedly, feeling that Shakespeare is utterly unaccountable and haphazard in his use of sources. What we should note, I think, is the profundity of Shakespeare's insight into romance structure which enabled him to see that Plautus' comedy and the recognition scene in the Apollonius romance were the beginning and the end of the same kind of story. The connecting links, which Shakespeare was clearly aware of, are, first, Plautus' *Amphitryon*, where the doubles are created by the magical power of gods, and, second, Apuleius, which seems to be glanced at in one remark in the dialogue: "If thou art chang'd to aught, 'tis to an ass." In the dark haunted forest of *A Midsummer Night's Dream*, the two heroes are not twins, but are as confused in their identity as though they were, and in this play again the metamorphosis into an ass recurs.

Shakespeare, like many other writers of comedy, often comes close to the *commedia dell'arte* convention, at the center of which is Harlequin. Of the various things Harlequin does, one is to divide himself into two people and hold dialogues with himself. He also sometimes dresses up as a woman, and sometimes plays a mute part—we shall come back to this mute figure in a moment. Another modulation of the twin theme, which also suggests a dreamer and the self he is dreaming about, occurs in the folktale of "The Two Brothers," which is in Grimm, and its literary developments. The latter include the medieval story of Amis and Amiloun. In this type of story one brother goes out on a quest or in search of adventure, the other remaining home, though able to tell from some sign how his brother is faring, and going into action when help is needed. This structural device is still useful in displaced stories where the look-alike twins are replaced by close friends, as in Scott's *Redgauntlet*.

On the lower reaches of descent we find the night world, often a dark and labyrinthine world of caves and shadows where the forest has turned subterranean, and where we are surrounded by the shapes of animals. If the meander-

and-descent patterns of paleolithic caves, along with the paintings on their walls, have anything like the same kind of significance, we are here retracing what are, so far as we know, the oldest imaginative steps of humanity.

Mythologies begin with creation myths, and creation myths are of two main types, depending on whether man is looking up or down from his middle earth when he is constructing it. If we look down, we see the cycle of animal and plant life, and creation myths suggested by this would most naturally be sexual ones, focusing eventually on some kind of earth-mother, the womb and tomb of all living things. If we look up, we see, not different forms of life emerging, but the same sun rising in the east. The cycle of the same, in Plato's phrase, suggests rather an artificial creation myth, a world made, not born, and made by a conscious and planning intelligence. Such a myth tends to be associated with a sky-father, who goes about his mysterious business without nursing his children. In sexual and earth-mother creation myths death does not have to be explained: death is built in to the whole process. But an intelligently made world could not have had any death or evil originally in it, so that a myth of fall is needed to complement it.

It is often assumed that the sexual and maternal myths are older, being more appropriate for an agricultural society, as their rivals were for the patriarchal, tool-using, urban society that came later. Certainly in Hesiod we gather that the sky-god we now have is a latecoming usurper and tyrant, the earth having sullenly retired below with her defeated titans. These subterranean titans, as that or as giants, persist all through romance. The artificial myth won out in our tradition, and the lower world became demonized, the usual fate of mythological losers. But many echoes of a very different feeling about the lower world linger in romance. Even in Grimm a lowerworld ogre may have a wife or mother who is willing to deceive him to help the hero.

Most of what goes on in the night world of romance is cruelty and horror, yet what is essential is not cruelty as such but the presence of some kind of ritual. In another Greek romance, *Ephesiaca*, by Xenophon of Ephesus, where the hero and heroine are called Habrocomes and Antheia, there is a series of demonic ordeals with a strong resemblance to those in the descent myths of the Bible, including the stories of Joseph and Daniel and the Passion of Christ. Many centuries later Chaucer, putting his heroine Constance, in *The Man of Law's Tale*, through similar tribulations, deliberately inserts the biblical parallels. There is no birth mystery in Xenophon's story, except that the junior leads are unreasonably beautiful: this makes the hero proud and boastful, and so he incurs the resentment of Eros. They are married at the beginning of the tale, and their future woes are summarized by an oracle. They take passage in a ship to try to avoid the forewarnings, but any reader of romances could have told them that that was a silly idea. The sailors get drunk, and the ship is captured by pirates. The drunkenness is a projection of the theme of the break in consciousness, and outlawed societies similar to these pirates are performing the same function in the smugglers of *Guy Mannering*, the Highland clans of *Rob Roy*, the bravos of Manzoni's *I promessi sposi*, the terrorist conspirators of Bulwer-Lytton's *Zanoni* and Wilkie Collins' *The Woman in White*, along with their twentieth-century successors. In Xenophon the captain is homosexually attracted to the hero and the first mate to the heroine, so that we are at no loss for the usual type of romantic suspense.

Habrocomes and Antheia are both sentenced to be

crucified; Antheia's sentence is commuted to being shut up in a pit with two mastiffs, whereupon the guard, who has the usual interest in her, feeds the mastiffs so that she comes to no harm. The resemblance to the story of Daniel in the lion's den is clear, and so is a parallel with the story of Absalom in a following episode, where Antheia is captured by a band of robbers who have a custom of hanging a victim from a tree and throwing javelins at him (in this case her). Antheia is strung up for this ordeal, but is rescued by a law-and-order group. Finally, weary of these amusements and of getting so many immodest proposals besides, Antheia asks a physician to give her a drug that will kill her. He gives her one that merely puts her to sleep, and as a result she is buried alive, with the traditional rituals of sacrificed victims and burned garments. She wakes up when liberated by grave robbers. This theme also occurs in the Apollonius story, and, with modifications, in Heliodorus: the archetype of death and rebirth, along with that of a descent to a lower world of graves and caves, is here present in one of its primary forms.

In the theme of the apparently dead and buried heroine who comes to life again, one of the themes of Shakespeare's *Cymbeline*, we seem to be getting a more undisplaced glimpse of the earth-mother at the bottom of the world. In later romance there is another glimpse of such a figure in Rider Haggard's *She*, a beautiful and sinister female ruler, buried in the depths of a dark continent, who is much involved with various archetypes of death and rebirth. In Xenophon of Ephesus the hero meets an old man who continues to love and live with his wife even though she has been embalmed as a mummy: similar themes are also in Haggard's story. Embalmed mummies suggest Egypt, which is preeminently the land of death and burial, and, largely because of its biblical role, of descent to a lower world.

This lower world is a world of increasing alienation and loneliness: the hero is not only separated from the heroine or his friends, but is often further isolated by being falsely accused of major crimes. The calumny of the hero is parallel to that of the calumniated mother or accused queen, but usually comes at a different stage of the total story. The hero is often a victim of what used to be called the badger game: an unscrupulous female tries to seduce him, and when he refuses sets up a cry that he has tried to rape her. This ordeal is part of Joseph's descent to Egypt in the Bible, and figures prominently in Heliodorus. Variations of it are still functional in *Tom Jones*, *The Moonstone*, and elsewhere, but it recedes in twentieth-century romance, in response to a convention that a male hero who would refuse sexual intercourse would be neither believable nor admirable.

Animal companions are frequent in descent themes, as part of the pattern of metamorphosis. Metamorphosis of the Ovidian type, where something that has been human or quasi-human becomes an object in the world of nature, represents the falling silent of the world in its paradisal or humanly intelligible phase. In our world man can no longer, in Blake's phrase, converse with animal forms of wisdom night and day. Sometimes the silent companion of the hero's descent is a ghost, the grateful dead man of a common folktale motif. One of the biblical descent stories, that of the Book of Tobit, has Tobias accompanied by a dog and by the angel Raphael, who is closely related structurally to the grateful dead man. The dog is a common lowerworld symbol: the hounds of the hunt, also, often represent the fact that animals may have more useful senses than human beings in this world. Human beings of the same structural type are often mute or inarticulate. Scott especially is fond of such figures: we have Lutin in *The Fortunes of Nigel*, the dumb dwarf who is Norna's servant in *The Pirate*, the dumb (or at any rate silent) girl in *Peveril of the Peak*, and Dominie Sampson in *Guy Mannering*, who knows all the standard Classical and modern languages even though he can barely speak himself. Ghosts and banshees attached to aristocratic families, like the White Lady in *The Monastery*, also belong to this oracular world. In naive romance, we have the folktale theme of the "bear's son," often portrayed as a lazy, powerful, awkward hero who may be driven from human society to seek solitude like a bear hibernating in a cave. The Icelandic hero Grettir the Strong is a hero of this type: he kills a bear in a cave behind a waterfall with the help of a companion named Björn (bear), whom he also kills a few pages further on. Parallels have been noted between Grettir's story and that of the much earlier *Beowulf*, in which the isolation of the hero is strongly marked. Beowulf descends to a mysterious submarine world in pursuit of Grendel's mother: his companions wait for him until noon, then disperse with no further inquiry.

Some of the paleolithic cave paintings mentioned earlier represent not only animals but what appear to be human beings in animal masks. In literature "such deliberate disguises," in Eliot's phrase, extend from the Homeric story of Circe to the beast-headed rout of Milton's *Comus* and beyond. In their total significance these figures are fertility spirits, part of the death-and-rebirth pattern of the lower world, but in the present context of descent, they represent chiefly Ovidian metamorphosis, the reducing of humanized beings to something subintelligent and subarticulate. In the Jonsonian masque they form the "antimasque" which begins the action, symbolizing the kind of chaos and disorder that is contrasted with the courtly occasion for the masque itself. A related motif of freezing into some kind of invariable pattern appears in many forms, including the paralysis which besets the Lady in *Comus,* as it did, much earlier, Theseus and Pirithous in Greek myth.

At lower levels the Narcissus or twin image darkens into a sinister doppelganger figure, the hero's shadow and the portent of his own death or isolation. In ordinary life there are two central data of experience that we cannot see without external assistance: our own faces and our own existence in time. To see the first we have to look in a mirror, and to see the second we have to look at the dial of a clock. The night world progressively becomes, as we sink deeper into it, a world where everything is an object, including ourselves, and consequently mirrors and clocks take on a good deal of importance as objectifying images. The classical romancers had to make do with doubles only, as the clock had not been invented. In more recent times, Poe is one of the hardiest explorers of this underworld region, and his fascination with clocks and pendulums and dial faces needs no elaboration. The mirror and twin themes in Poe branch out into various doppelganger formulas, as in *William Wilson* and *The Imp of the Perverse.*

The reflection of one's personality may take the form of a container where the hero's soul or life is kept, and of such objects the closest to the central Narcissus theme is the portrait, as we have it in Oscar Wilde's *Picture of Dorian Gray* and elsewhere. Doubles in time are, of course, much more complicated than doubles in space: the great pioneer work here is Henry James' unfinished *The Sense of the Past,* and the doubles produced by some kind of "time machine" have been extensively explored in science fiction. We can also have such mirror devices as that of Gide's *The Counterfeiters,* a book about a man who is writing a book called *The Counterfeiters.* We may note that this device is

already present in *Paradise Lost*, where the final fall of
Adam includes his being absorbed into, and told the story
of, the book which is later on to start with him.

At the bottom of the night world we find the cannibal
feast, the serving up of a child or lover as food, which we
have in the Greek stories of Thyestes and Tereus, and later
Provençal legends incorporated into Pound's *Cantos*. Such
a theme is important not for its horrific frisson, but as the
image which causes that frisson, the identifying of human
and animal natures in a world where animals are food for
man. Such a theme merges readily with the theme of human sacrifice in its most undisplaced form, which is the
swallowing of a youth or maiden by a subterranean or
submarine monster. St. George, Perseus, Rogero in Ari-
osto, and many other heroes save virgins from this fate;
Theseus puts an end to the offering of young Athenians to
the Minotaur in the underground labyrinth of Crete; the
brothers of Bluebeard's last wife put an end to the series of
slaughtered brides. In most versions of the Bluebeard
story, and elsewhere, the victims are allowed to escape or
revive: this happens even to the fifty children swallowed
by the subterranean demon in William Beckford's *Vathek*.

The birth of the divine hero, we remember from Yeats,
is often symbolized by the conjunction of a divine bird and
a human woman. At the furthest remove from this we find
a demonic parody of the same image, the bestial conjunction, usually, of a male animal and a human female. Thus
the Minotaur was the result of the impregnating of Pasi-
phae by a bull. In Apuleius the nadir, so to speak, of the
main action of the story comes at a point where a woman
is condemned as a whore, and, as her judges have discovered unusual aptitudes in the ass who is the transformed
Lucius, the ass is ordered to have public intercourse with
her. It is the peculiarity of this scene that its fantastic set-

ting is what gives it its essential horror. Granted that asses cannot be trained to do this sort of thing, still, if they could be so trained, that is undoubtedly what the human race would be most interested in training them to do.

If we may now pull together these descent motifs and see what their undisplaced form is, the descending hero or heroine is going down into a dark and labyrinthine world of caves and shadows which is also either the bowels and belly of an earth-monster, or the womb of an earth-mother, or both. A female monster of this type appears in a Mesopotamian myth as Tiamat, the primeval creature whose body formed the creation. The same motif is slightly displaced in stories where a hero kills a dragon who guards a treasure hoard, like Fafnir in the Sigurd saga. The undisplaced, or death-and-rebirth, form of the dragon quest is a descent through his open mouth into his belly and back out again, the theme that appears in the biblical story of Jonah and is later applied to Christ's descent to hell. In the interests of general decorum, Christ and Jonah are assumed to be returning by the same route: we may however compare Dante, who also enters the "mouth" of hell, and reaches the end of it at the Satanic rectum. A very slightly more undisplaced version of this would identify hell with the body of Satan, so that Dante would not only enter his mouth but be excreted from the other end, becoming as a result what Carlyle would call a Diogenes Teufelsdröckh, a god-born devil's dung.

I mention this because the mythological universe is, in one of its aspects, a gigantic or macrocosmic body, with analogies to the human body. The stars, sun, and moon present an analogy to a human brain, especially when they are taken to be images of the intelligence of a creating god. At the bottom of this macrocosmic world we find the organs of generation and of excretion, which are emphasized in proportion as this part of the mythical universe is made demonic. Devils are associated with blackness, soot, and sulfurous smell, besides having the horns, hoofs, and tails of the sort of fertility spirit that is close to the sexual instinct.

The radical of satire, as Lucian established long ago, is a descent narrative, where we enter a lower world which reveals the sources of human absurdity and folly. Most great satirists, including Swift, Rabelais, and Joyce, have understood very well that most of these sources are to be located in the abdominal, genital, and excretory regions, a fact emphasized in modern psychology but not discovered by it, as the etymology of such words as hypochondria and hysteria makes clear. *Gulliver's Travels* reminds us that we recurrently find in this lower world very little people and very big people. The latter include the giants who are related to the titans in Hesiod's story of the defeated earth-mother: they are usually stupid and easily deceived giants, but sometimes, notably in Rabelais, we are reminded of the exuberant strength that lies suppressed, for the most part, in our lower bodily areas. The little people appear as gnomes, dwarfs, and similar types of earth spirit. Sometimes the same identity changes from one to the other: thus the immense devils of the first book of *Paradise Lost* shrink into tiny fairies at the end of the book.

As winter turns to spring, nature shows a power of regaining her youth that does not exist for individual human life. Robert Graves tells us that his earth-mother, whom he calls the white goddess, originally renewed her virginity every spring: the impossibility of this in human experience is one reason for the emphasis on preserving virginity in romance. A great deal of literary and religious imagination is concerned with the effort to assimilate and identify individual human life with natural rebirth. Explorers of the New World were often more interested in fountains of youth than in anything they actually found, and the search for prolonged youth is still a theme of romance in, for example, Bulwer-Lytton's *A Strange Story*. The buried treasure hoard guarded by a dragon, full of gold and jewels (which are of subterranean origin in any case), affords an obvious motive for a descent quest. But much more important in early societies is the quest for renewed fertility, and sometimes, as in Ruskin's thoroughly traditional fairy tale, "The King of the Golden River," we realize that the release of the life-giving powers that come with the spring and the rain is the authentic form of the treasure hoard. The Fafnir figure, the dragon guarding the hoard, is in that case lineally descended from the sea monster of many myths who has swallowed all the water in the world, and continues to devour all the youth and beauty it can get.

The fertility of the land and the virility of the king who rules it have an ancient magical connection, and the link between natural and sexual vitality appears in such images as the lance and grail of the Percival legend, which, according to Jessie Weston, were originally magical food-providers. Lance and grail, at least in the Grail's developed form as a chalice or cup, have an analogy to male and female genital organs. Milton's *Comus* gives us a Christian and demonized view of this aspect of the descent: Comus is the son of Circe; he attempts a sexual seduction designed to break the Lady's connection with the higher world of chastity, and his chief emblems are a wand and a cup. Similarly, the replacing of an aged and impotent king by a youthful successor is really a displacement of the theme of renewing the old king's youth. Hence many descent themes, from the Harrowing of Hell to the psychological quests of

Freud and his successors, center on the theme of the release, revival, or reemergence of parental figures buried in a world of amnesia or suppressed memory. In romance the descent theme often has a great deal to do with one's descent in the genealogical sense, where the crucial event is the discovery of the real relation between the chief characters and their parents. Sometimes we simply have a death and revival of parental figures, as at the conclusion of Sidney's *Arcadia*, where the king has been given a sleeping potion by his queen, and comes to life in the middle of a trial of the two young heroes on the charge of having murdered him. We may compare the oracle scene in *Cymbeline*, and the appearance of parental figures there.

When it is wisdom that is sought in the lower world, it is almost always wisdom connected with the anxiety of death in some form or other, along with the desire to know what lies beyond. Such wisdom, however displaced, is usually communicated in some kind of dark saying, and riddles and ciphers and oracular utterances of all kinds proliferate around the end of the descending journey. They are naturally prominent in Poe, with his fondness for this area, and one appears at the end of the wanderings of Arthur Gordon Pym. It is not very helpful: Keats's Endymion is more fortunate, and gets fairly specific advice about how the poet's imagination should put together the world he has been traversing.

Here again we go back to very ancient imaginative patterns, such as the Egyptian myth of the underworld judgment, with its weighing of the heart, its negative confessions of the "I am not a crook" type, and its separation of souls into those who pass into the world of Osiris and those who are devoured by a crocodile. This lowerworld judgment is in marked contrast to the upperworld apocalypses in Christianity and elsewhere: institutional Christianity gets them mixed up, but the poetic imagination knows the difference. The upperworld is essentially a form of revelation or full knowledge: in the underworld the central figure is not only a prisoner and accused, but he himself knows nothing and yet is known.

The horror of being totally known is so great that most romances evade it by the device of a trial founded on an unjust, malicious, or mistaken charge, which the hero or heroine avoids by the revelation of his or her real identity. This means that the trial presupposes a wrong identity. But occasionally, as in Kafka's *The Trial*, the primitive fear returns. Even in the most displaced and farcical forms of the theme, such as the ordeal of the blindfolded Parolles in *All's Well*, we glimpse something about an involuntarily acquired self-knowledge that is more terrible than death itself. The symbol of this hostile knowledge is generally some form of scales or balance, the emblem of the law, and a sinister emblem because it quantifies, so to speak, all the elements of life that we feel cannot or ought not to be weighed or measured. Most romances keep well out of the way of such emblems, and provide instead various superficial modulations of it which assist the escape of the chief characters. One peculiarly silly example, which I am forced to mention because it occurs so often in romance, is the virgin-detecting gadget, the machine which proves that the heroine really is one in spite of everything, and which appears at the end of Heliodorus and Achilles Tatius. It survives in the girdle of Florimell in Spenser's *Faerie Queene* and elsewhere.

It is possible never to get out of this lower world, and some may not even want to. For it may also assume the form of a false paradise, like Spenser's Bower of Bliss. Of those turned into animals by Circe, some might refuse to return to human shape—this theme was a popular Renaissance paradox. Or there may even be genuine paradises in the lower world, descending from the Classical Elysium, or at least places of contentment, like the underworld community that we meet in the last part of Herbert Read's *The Green Child.* Sometimes, too, the descent imagery is merely playful, as in many children's stories.

Yet even in *Alice in Wonderland* the tone is curiously ambiguous. Alice descends in pursuit of a rabbit preoccupied with the dial of his watch: she is not, like Dante in the *Inferno,* traversing a cone from base to apex, but a spiral-shaped poem, ending in the word "death," appears later in the story. There is a good deal of alienation in Alice's world: she is never quite sure of her own identity, and the continuity with her previous life is broken when her carefully memorized poems turn into grotesque parodies. Giants and dwarfs, we saw, inhabit the lower world: Alice is always either too big or too small, hence often a nuisance or an unwanted guest. She feels estranged from her body by her changes of size, and falls into a pool of what a post-Victorian reader would simply call her liquid excretions. A sinister beheading queen makes her appearance, and the theme of metamorphosis is introduced in the witches' kitchen of the ugly duchess, where a little boy turns into a pig, not that Lewis Carroll would have considered that much of a metamorphosis. The story ends in a trial in which all the characters present turn on the heroine. We notice the prominence of cards in the story: cards and dice are common in descent narratives, because of their overtones of fatality and chance.

The only companion who accompanies us to the end of the descent is the demonic accuser, who takes the form of the accusing memory. The memory is demonic here because it has forgotten only one thing, the original identity of what it accompanies. It conveys to us the darkest knowledge at the bottom of the world, the vision of the absurd, the realization that only death is certain, and that nothing before or after death makes sense. The white goddess may sweep on to a renewed life, take another lover, and forget her past, but man can neither forget nor renew. But although in a world of death nothing is more absurd than life, life is the counter-absurdity that finally defeats death. And in a life that is a pure continuum, beginning with a birth that is a random beginning, ending with a death that is a random ending, nothing is more absurd than telling stories that do begin and end. Yet this is part of the counter-absurdity of human creation, the vision that comes, like the vision of the *Bhagavadgita*, to alienated figures on a battlefield of dying men, and ends with finding one's identity in the body of the god of gods who also contains the universe.

In William Morris' *The Earthly Paradise,* a group of lonely old men from Classical and Northern worlds gather on an island and exchange the traditional tales that they have known from childhood. It seems the most futile of activities, the work of disillusionment, weariness, and exhaustion, almost of senility. Even the designer of the whole enterprise calls himself "the idle singer of an empty day." And yet, we read in the "Epilogue" that they are not simply putting in the time until they die: they are fighting a battle against death, with some dim understanding that the telling and retelling of the great stories, in the face of the accusing memory, is a central part of the only battle that there is any point in fighting:

> And these folk—these poor tale-tellers, who strove
> In their wild way the heart of Death to move,
> E'en as we singers, and failed, e'en as we,—
> Surely on their side I at least will be,

And deem that when at last, their fear worn out,
They fell asleep, all that old shame and doubt
Shamed them not now, nor did they doubt it good,
That they in arms against that Death had stood.

One thinks of one of the greatest figures of romance, Scheherezade, telling her thousand and one tales so that the suspense of each tale may keep her alive for one more night. Perhaps even the storytellers in Boccaccio's *Decameron* are not simply running away from the plague that rages outside their walls. "Once upon a time": the formula invokes, out of a world where nothing remains, something older than history, younger than the present moment, always willing and able to descend again once more.

5

Quis Hic Locus?
Themes of Ascent

5

WE IDENTIFIED TWO types of descent themes: those that descend from a higher world to this one and those that descend from this world to a lower one. The general theme of descent, we saw, was that of a growing confusion of identity and of restrictions on action. There is a break in consciousness at the beginning, with analogies to falling asleep, followed by a descent to a lower world which is sometimes a world of cruelty and imprisonment, sometimes an oracular cave. In the descent there is a growing isolation and immobility: charms and spells hold one motionless; human beings are turned into subhuman creatures, and made more mechanical in behavior; hero or heroine are trapped in labyrinths or prisons. The narrative themes and images of ascent are much the same in reverse, and the chief conceptions are those of escape, remembrance, or discovery of one's real identity, growing freedom, and the breaking of enchantment. Again there are two major narrative divisions: the ascent from a lower world and the ascent to a higher world.

As the hero or heroine enters the labyrinthine lower world, the prevailing moods are those of terror or uncritical awe. At a certain point, perhaps when the strain, as the storyteller doubtless hopes, is becoming unbearable, there may be a revolt of the mind, a recovered detachment, the typical expression of which is laughter. The ambiguity of the oracle becomes the ambiguity of wit, something addressed to a verbal understanding that shakes the mind free. This point is also marked by generic changes from the tragic and ironic to the comic and satiric. Thus in Rabelais the huge giants, the search for an oracle, and other lower-world themes that in different contexts would be frightening or awe-inspiring, are presented as farce. *Finnegans Wake* in our day also submerges us in a dream world of mysterious oracles, but when we start to read the atmosphere changes, and we find ourselves surrounded by jokes and puns. Centuries earlier, the story was told of how Demeter wandered over the world in fruitless search of her lost daughter Proserpine, and sat lonely and miserable in a shepherd's hut until the obscene jests and raillery of the servant girl Iambe and the old nurse Baubo finally persuaded her to smile. The Eleusinian mysteries which Demeter established were solemn and awful rites of initiation connected with the renewal of the fertility cycle; but Iambe and Baubo helped to ensure that there would also be comic parodies of them, like Aristophanes' *Frogs*. According to Plutarch, those who descended to the gloomy cave of the oracle of Trophonius might, after three days, recover the power of laughter.

In an atmosphere of tragic irony the emphasis is on spellbinding, linked to a steady advance of paralysis or death; in an atmosphere of comedy, we break through this inevitable advance by a device related to the riddle, an explanation of a mystery. Such an explanation, which usually takes the form of a recognition scene, transforms a story into a kind of game. That is, the story becomes a puzzle, of which the recognition scene is the solution. The fact that it is usually a rather easy, not to say transparent, puzzle does not affect this. The ideal is a reversal of movement which is both a surprise to the reader and yet seems to him an inevitable development of events up to that point. This ideal has never been attained by any work of literature, and even if it were, it would seem to us at best only a triumph of ingenuity. The reason for this melancholy situation is that a completely successful comic resolution depends upon an ideal reader or listener, which means one who has never encountered a comedy or romance before, and has no idea of literary convention. We notice that where complex explanations are required in Shakespearean comedy, they are sometimes postponed until *after* the end of the play, when the audience, who knows more about such things than the characters, will not be there to hear them. What is really recognized is simply the cyclical movement of the story, down through the threatening complications and up again through the escape from them, not the particular mystery by which this movement may be operated.

We can see this more clearly in comic stories where there is no effort at surprise, and where the recognition has been visible throughout. In *The Earthly Paradise* Morris tells the story of "The Man Born To Be King," the theme of which is summarized in the argument: "It was foretold to a great king, that he who should reign after him should be lowborn and poor; which thing came to pass in the end, for all that the king could do." The old king makes the most desperate efforts to exterminate the coming new one, who relentlessly grows from infant to youth to man, turning up at intervals to remind the king of the uselessness of his efforts. In such a story there is no "suspense"; we know from the beginning that the infant's survival is predestined, and we simply watch its progress. The progress is rationalized in the story by appeals to fate, to the prophecy of an oracular wise man, and to the conjunctions of the stars. Morris is unlikely to have "believed" in fate or prophecy or astrology, nor need the reader. What entertains us is the archetype of death and rebirth, where the growing new life takes over the feelings of the irresistible and inevitable which are normally attached to death. The same principle operates in rescue scenes, in impossible tasks, which we know will somehow be accomplished, in unanswerable riddles which we know will somehow be answered. The feeling that death is inevitable comes to us from ordinary experience; the feeling that new life is inevitable comes to us from myth and fable. The latter is therefore both more true and more important.

Such themes in romance are often linked with the providential framework of the Christian universe which is contemporary with so much of it. Thus Sidney, at the beginning of the fourth book of the *Arcadia:*

The almighty wisdom evermore delighting to show the world, that by unlikeliest means greatest matters may come to conclusion: that human reason may be the more humbled, and more willingly give place to divine providence: as at the first it brought in *Damaetas* to play a part in this royal pageant, so having continued him still an actor, now that all things were grown ripe for an end, made his folly the instrument of revealing that, which far greater cunning had sought to conceal.

Damaetas is a ridiculous clown, and we are reminded of the comment about the blundering Dogberry and his cohorts in *Much Ado:* "What your wisdoms could not discover, these shallow fools have brought to light." The echo from the New Testament emphasizes the parallel between comic and Christian myths. In the earlier version of Sidney's story generally known as the Old Arcadia, the passage corresponding to the one quoted contains the words: "So evil a ground doth evil stand upon, and so manifest it is, that nothing remains strongly, but that which hath the good foundation of goodness." Such passages remind us that the technical devices of storytelling are not simply responses to popular demand, which hardly existed for Sidney in any case, but the result of working within a certain kind of mythological framework.

There is a little more narrative suspense in the Houdini motif, where hero or heroine wriggle out of their prisons by themselves. The great exemplar here is the escape of Ulysses from the cave of Polyphemus, which contains most of the archetypes of this episode. The prison is often controlled by one of the giants who inhabit the lower reaches of the night world, and in less displaced romances he is often a cannibal giant. Front-de-Boeuf in *Ivanhoe*, to whose castle we shall come in a moment, is often referred to as gigantic. In the Polyphemus story Ulysses gets out by being mistaken for a sheep, more or less: in other words the assimilation of human and animal forms is still present. In more displaced fiction a similar Polyphemus figure could be a Dickensian grotesque threatening to devour or pollute the heroine, like Gride in *Nicholas Nickleby* or Uriah Heep in *David Copperfield*. The word "grotesque," incidentally, always carries with it something of its "grotto" or lowerworld connections. More often the displaced imprisoning giant is a jealous father, who locks up the heroine.

The ingenuity shown by the escaping character represents very often a triumph of what we have been calling *froda*, wiliness or craft. When it is purely that, we are being shown a triumph of evil, as in the escape of Medea in Euripides. More usually, deception and theft and disguise are enlisted in a good cause. In the progress from darkness

blindness & progress

darkness — light

to light, which is the area covered by this phase, we find the myths of the origin of fire, which are usually myths of stealing it. Similarly, blindness, or living in the dark, is often associated with the world of the giant which is being escaped from, as again in the Polyphemus story. In the Book of Genesis blindness and animal disguise themes are combined in the story of the deception of the blind Isaac by Jacob, who covers his smooth hands with the skin of an animal to pass as the rough and hairy Esau. In Chaucer's *Merchant's Tale* the cuckolded husband has his sight restored by an outraged deity, but his wife manages to persuade him that he really is blind after all. In a more genial setting, even Jane Eyre's Rochester has something of the blind giant about him at the end of the story: the restoring of his sight is a symbol of his evolution from pursuing lover to Victorian husband. Because of the frequency of the convention of escape, we may sometimes feel that there is something illusory about the dungeon or whatever: however dark and thick-walled, it seems bound to turn into a womb of rebirth sooner or later. This theme is clearest when the romance has allegorical overtones, as in the prison of Orgoglio in *The Faerie Queene* or of Giant Despair in *The Pilgrim's Progress*. There is also in this case some connection with the atmosphere of a nightmare, from which one can always escape by waking up.

The conventional happy ending of romance may seem to us faked, manipulated, or thrown in as a contemptuous concession to a weak-minded reader. In our day ironic modes are the preferred ones for serious fiction, and of course if the real conception of a work of fiction is ironic, a conventionally happy ending would be forced, or, in extreme cases, dishonest. But if the conception is genuinely romantic and comic, the traditional happy ending is usually the one that fits. It is obvious however both that the happy ending exists only for readers who finish the book, and, within the book, only for characters who survive to the end of the story. Such characters are apt to expound a good deal on the benevolence of whatever power got them out of their predicaments, and we may sometimes feel that this shows some insensitivity to the fates of the subordinate characters who perished on the way.

In *Ivanhoe* much of the action takes place in Front-de-Boeuf's castle, where terrible things almost go on. A Jew is going to be tortured to make him give up his money; his daughter and another heroine are being threatened with rape. They all escape relatively unharmed, but in the actual Middle Ages there were many people who went through such ordeals without escaping. Scott even interrupts his narrative to show how true this was, by quoting a passage from the Anglo-Saxon Chronicle. He also provides foils for his two heroines. Rowena gets out of the castle, but another Saxon woman previously abducted did not; Rebecca escapes a trial for sorcery on the ground that her medical skill is witchcraft, but another Jewess, from whom she had learned her skill, was actually martyred on the same pretext. It seems clear that appeals to God, by virtuous characters threatened with evil, may be of little use unless God has a secretary to handle such calls in the form of a good-natured novelist, backed by a sentimental public.

The happy endings of life, as of literature, exist only for survivors. When confronted with something profoundly evil in life like the Nazi regime in Germany, we may say that after all it did collapse in a few years. This fact was of no help to the millions of people it tortured and murdered before it fell, and yet it is true, however smug it may sound, that the survivors have the more complete perspective. Hence the modern world may accept comic mythologies, such as the progress myth in the democracies and the classless society myth of Marxism, although the benefits of such happy endings are only for those living in a remote future. One of the things that comedy and romance as a whole are about, clearly, is the unending, irrational, absurd persistence of the human impulse to struggle, survive, and where possible escape. It is perhaps worth noting how intense is the desire of most readers of romances for the happy ending. In *Ivanhoe*, once more, a subordinate character named Athelstane, whom most readers would hardly care much about, is killed off, but was brought to life again because of objections made to Scott by a reader. Scott's complaisance in this matter strikes us, in our ironic age, as a trifle meretricious, but, again, we may be judging by the wrong conventions. Even the desire to be reborn in a happier future may be more deep-seated than we think. In Morris' *News from Nowhere* the calmness with which the inhabitants of that happy future world accept their nineteenth-century "Guest" perhaps suggests that, like the inhabitants of the Christian heaven, they would expect people from an earlier and sadder time to be reborn into it.

The standard escape device of romance is that of escape through a shift of identity, the normal basis of the recognition scene. As a rule the recognition scene involves producing some equivalent of a birth certificate, which causes the action to return to the point of the hero's or heroine's birth. As this is usually a time many years before the story begins, we have two interlocking rhythms of time, one the time of the narrative action, the other a much more deliberate and creative time in which hidden truths are eventually brought to light. Certain folktale themes, such as the hare-and-tortoise race in Aesop and the similar race of Atalanta, who loses to her suitor because he throws golden balls in front of her to distract her attention, remind us that in the conventions of comedy and comic romance, at least, the slower and more leisurely rhythms of time are the ones that win out in the end.

Such a discovery about birth is usually accompanied or followed by a marriage. Tragedy, or threatening tragic complications in romance, often involve stresses within families, such as a father's overbearing will or the threat of incestuous relationship. In the love-and-honor conflicts so frequent in romantic stories, the imperatives of honor usually have to do with attachments to family, tribal, or class loyalties. Tragedy often results from the inability to break with these. Even Mark Antony's primary "duty" is to remain a Roman in the family of Caesar, as Cleopatra sardonically notes. It seems intolerably simplistic to explain all forms of nightmare by the fear of incest, as some Freudians do, yet incest is certainly a central theme in nightworld imagery, and the transfer of energies and affections from one's family to the new family of a marriage is the easiest kind of comic resolution. A comic resolution, in fact, could almost be defined as an action that breaks out of the Oedipus ring, the destruction of a family or other close-knit social group by the tensions and jealousies of its members.

The next stage of ascent is the separation between the lower world and those who are destined to escape from it. Again we start with an act of conscious detachment, one that takes the form of recognizing the demonic as demonic. The detective story is a genre directed toward this kind of recognition. The detective story is, in a comic context, an epiphany of law, a balancing and neutralizing activity in society, the murderer discovered at the end balancing the corpse that we normally find at the beginning. Devotees of detective stories tell me that there is usually a sense of anticlimax when the murderer is identified, an anticlimax only resolved by reaching for another story. One implication of this is that law is not justice, though at its best it may point in the direction of justice. In literature, as in life, the only real justice is poetic justice, and the story of the triumph of law does not quite achieve this.

In any case the detective story operates, for the most part, in a deeply conservative social area, where the emphasis is on reintegrating the existing order. Its vogue was contemporary with realism. Fiction in the last generation or so has turned increasingly from realism to fantasy, partly because fantasy is the normal technique for fiction writers who do not believe in the permanence or continuity of the society they belong to. Similarly, the detective story, as a ritual game which the powers of law and order always win, has modulated to a type of thriller with much more anarchic social overtones. The usual conservative tendency in comedy is to move from subjective illusion to an acceptance of the standards of society, as a superior norm. Thus in Jane Austen's *Emma*, the novel in which her early burlesques of romance forms paid off, Emma imposes a romance pattern on her friend Harriet, whose parentage is unknown, and who therefore, by all the rules of romance, must be of some quite exceptional birth. Emma's discovery that Harriet is, in parentage as well as character, pretty well what she appears to be is the discovery that liberates her from illusion.

In *Sense and Sensibility* we have a more somber study of a progress toward social reality in the mind of Marianne, who is, at least structurally, the central figure of the story. Marianne's sensibility is of a polarizing kind that divides people into those like herself, who cannot and should not try to control their emotions, and those who, like her sister Elinor, are so calm as to have no emotions. Following a disappointment in love, her sensibility drives her into an illness which it has directly created. She recognizes this when she recovers from it, and remarks that if she had died she would have been guilty of self-destruction. After her recovery she adopts the genuine form of the same polarization, the contrast between the sensibility she had indulged and the sense which Elinor had shown all along. I mention this book here because it illustrates so clearly the contrast we have already spoken of, between what an individual story may present and what the convention it belongs to may present. Every so often we have had glimpses of an inherently revolutionary quality in romance, however conservative the individual stories may be, and the polarizing element in Marianne's mind indicates a place where we may pick up a clue to it.

We noticed that the trial scene which is common at or near the end of a romance is usually an unjust trial, one that proceeds on false assumptions. Or, as in the Chinese play *The Chalk Circle*, we may have two trial scenes, one before a foolish judge and one before a wiser one, to represent the progress from illusion to reality. In such stories illusion is an attribute of society as a whole rather than of an individual. Such a society sets up a perverted order, sometimes, as in the *Odyssey*, during the absence of a genuine ruler whose return puts an end to it. The process of escaping from such a society may involve a complete social *culbute* or overturn, separating and opposing the liberated forces from the enslaving ones. Revolutionary attitudes are dialectical and polarizing attitudes, and this involves, in romance, the identifying of the demonic or regressive and its clear separation from whatever is progressive in the story. In romance it is much more frequently the individual, the hero or heroine, who has the vision of liberation, and the society they are involved with that wants to remain in a blind and gigantic darkness. In the *Odyssey*, the containing form is still a conservative one, but even there we notice how the gradual emergence of the disguised Ulysses in the household tends to polarize the characters, those who have to be destroyed at the end having already condemned themselves by their attitudes.

We found that in descent narratives the central image is that of metamorphosis, the freezing of something human and conscious into an animal or plant or inanimate object. Ascent themes introduce us to the opposite kind of metamorphosis, the growing of identity through the casting off of whatever conceals or frustrates it. The simplest form of such ascending metamorphosis is the removal of enchantment, in which an animal disguise or something parallel is replaced by the original human form. The frog becomes the prince; Lucius the ass, in Apuleius, becomes Lucius the initiate of Isis; the Wife of Bath's loathly lady, having got what she wanted, becomes a beautiful lady. Closely related is the comic theme of release from a humor, where a character with a mechanical pattern of behavior is able to become free of it.

We are now coming, by the same reverse movement, into the area of the twins or doppelganger figures who are so prominent in descent imagery. The theme now before us is that of the separating of the demonic principle from its opposite, when the two closely resemble each other. An early Christian romance known as the Clementine Recognitions features a hero named Clement, identified with a famous early Christian apostle and writer, who attaches himself to the more famous St. Peter, and follows him in his evangelical wanderings. Clement is the son of parents who have become separated through a slandered-mother situation: Clement's uncle had designs on his mother, who left home, taking her twin sons with her. Clement, the third son, remained at home with the father until the father left in search of the mother and also disappeared. The mother, of course, was shipwrecked and separated from the twins. In the course of the story, or what there is of a story, the family is picked up in stages. First, a beggar woman living in the greatest poverty and misery is discovered by Peter, and is identified as the mother. He has to supply hands for her by a miracle first, because she has gnawed them off for hunger. Students of folktale say that the accused-mother motif is closely related to another known as "the maiden without hands," an association which may be the original reason for this bizarre detail.

Peter and his entourage then go to Antioch, where there are two prominent Christians who "turn out to be" the twins. They were captured by pirates, no less, at the time of the shipwreck and were sold to a Jewess who was a Christian proselyte. In the neighborhood is an old man who is an astrologer and believes in fate and the origin of everything in natural causes. Peter cures him of these theological errors and he is shown to be the long lost father, whose name is Faustus. Evidently this story of a reuniting family is intended as some sort of allegory of the Last Judgment, which for the author and his readers, members of the family of God, will be one vast recognition scene.

We notice that the mother has twin sons: they have changed their names, just to make it harder, but nothing is otherwise made of this feature, which is doubtless taken over from an earlier story. On the other hand, there is a strong emphasis on the theme of the demonic double. Peter's great opponent all through the story is Simon Magus the enchanter, and in connection with him Peter remarks that God has appointed for this world certain pairs, the one coming first being evil and the second good. He gives ten examples of these pairs, beginning with Cain and Abel and ending with Antichrist and Christ. One of these ten pairs is Simon Magus and Simon Peter. At the end of the story Simon Magus, through his enchantments, implants his own face on Faustus. Peter promises to remove this false face if Faustus will go to the marketplace in his Simon Magus appearance and make a speech renouncing the latter's point of view and defending the Christian one. Faustus does and Peter does, and all ends happily.

This rather childish conclusion seems to be again an allegory of the annihilation of error through consolidating and defining it as the opposite or parody of the truth. In short, the Clementine Recognitions, as its title implies, passes over the theme of confused identity in the twins, who are not confusing anybody in spite of the change of names, and focuses on the opposite theme of demonic resemblance. The story of Barlaam and Josaphat, mentioned earlier, also introduces the theme of a demonic double, an antagonist of Christianity who looks exactly like a defender of it, and employs it with an equally earnest clumsiness. Such devices in Christian stories reflect the revolutionary and dialectical element in Christian belief, which is constantly polarizing its truth against the falsehoods of the heathen, but, like other revolutionary doctrines, feels most secure when the dark side takes the form of a heresy that closely resembles itself. In secular literature the theme of the separating of a character from a demonic shadow or double may be as rudimentary as these examples or as subtle and complex as Conrad's *Secret Sharer*.

We have already come across the device of the doubled heroine, sometimes represented by a dark and a fair girl, sometimes linked to a grave-and-gay contrast of temperament. Often we have two sisters, the older one dark and haughty, the younger one fair and milder. The two heroines of the *Arcadia* follow this pattern, which is a commonplace in Victorian fiction: it even occurs in *Huckleberry Finn*, with the Grangerford sisters. We saw that in this arrangement one girl is sometimes heading for the choice of one of her suitors and marriage to him, the other for virginity or devotion to a cause, and that this device helps to produce the two major cadences of romance, the allegro one and the penseroso one. Sometimes the dark heroine has a suggestion of the demonic about her, as in the Miriam of Hawthorne's *Marble Faun*; sometimes, as with the Cora of *The Last of the Mohicans*, one girl is killed off mainly to clear her out of the way so that the hero can marry the other in a monogamous society. In *The Castle of Otranto* the more interesting of two heroines is similarly eliminated to fulfill a prophecy about the extinction of her father's line. In such situations there may be a slight suggestion that one girl is a displaced sacrificial object whose death prolongs or renews the other's life. In Dickens we have, in a male setting, an explicit use of this theme in the martyrdom of Sydney Carton at the end of *A Tale of Two Cities*.

This device has a long ancestry in romances where the heroine is doubled with another figure who has so much less of the reader's sympathy that he does not mind much if she gets killed. In Heliodorus there is a treacherous go-between named Thisbe, who appears in the story when the heroine Chariclea is hidden in a cave by an Egyptian robber named Thamyris. Thamyris, seeing that his fortunes are apparently lost, goes into the cave to murder Chariclea. Heliodorus explains, in a comment alluded to by Shakespeare, that it is the custom of "barbarians," in desperate straits, to kill the person they most love in order to have company in the next world: similar themes have met us earlier. Thamyris enters the cave, finds Thisbe there with her back turned to him, and stabs her, thinking her to be Chariclea. The hero Theagenes then enters, finds Thisbe lying on her face, also assumes her to be Chariclea, and utters a long lament about the cruelty of fortune. Being a hero in a romance, he completes the lament before he turns her over. The fact that Thisbe resembles Chariclea so closely, at least from behind (later on Chariclea's voice is mistaken for Thisbe's), makes her a shadow or demonic double of the heroine. Whatever barbarians may do, it is often convenient for a romancer to have such a figure to kill off, to provide a death-and-rebirth displacement for the heroine.

We often have too, in softer lighting, contrasted groupings of progressive and regressive characters, who forward or retard the festive conclusion. In Scott there are quite elaborate constructions of this kind, generally of female figures. In *The Pirate* there is a sibyl named Norna, who believes that she can control the weather and predict the future. She has doubts about her abilities, but she is sane enough, not merely to ask herself whether she is sane, but to decide to stay mad, on the ground that it's more fun that way. She is, of course, "cured" in the last chapter, because in romance all magicians, whatever the reality of their powers, have to renounce their magic at the end. Norna is the mother of the pirate: she thinks, however, that she is the mother of the hero, and is anxious for the latter to marry Minna, the wrong or regressive heroine, because she herself represents that function in the plot. Thus she has the displaced role of a magician who constructs, not the total action, like Prospero in *The Tempest*, but the regressive part of the action, like Archimago in *The Faerie Queene*, an enchantment that the surviving characters must break free from.

This polarizing of action is obvious enough in romance; but the test of every revolutionary movement, however

romantic, comes when it must establish continuity with
what has preceded it. We remember that a romance often
begins with a break in consciousness or loss of memory: in
ascent imagery, then, we should expect a third stage, following the recognition of the demonic and its separation
from the progressive or surviving elements, which would
be the restoring of the broken current of memory. The
theme of restoring the memory is, naturally, often an element in the recognition scene itself, as the action then normally returns to the beginning of the story and interprets it
more truly than the previous account has done. The favorite device employed is what I call a talisman of recognition, some emblem or object, a birthmark on the body,
tokens put beside an exposed infant, and the like, which
symbolizes the original identity.

In the nineteenth century, theories about an unconscious
mind that never really forgets anything were starting to be
developed, and such a mind supplies a possible setting for
the recovery of a lost memory. In several Victorian romances a situation recurs in which the key to the recognition is held in the memory of someone who does not know
that he or she possesses it. Thus a good deal of the action
of Wilkie Collins' *The Woman in White* turns on a secret
concealed in the damaged brain of a madwoman, one
which relates to the social origin of the villain who has
married the heroine. In Sheridan LeFanu's *House by the
Churchyard*, which is closer to the conventional detective
story, the mystery about the identity of the villain is
locked inside the unconscious brain of the man the villain
had nearly murdered, and a trepanning operation is attempted to dig out the memory.

In Wilkie Collins' story there is a dog who has taken a
strong dislike to the plausible villain, according to a common principle of romance which may be called "dog

knows." After great efforts it is finally established that the mystery surrounding the villain is the fact that he was not a gentleman by birth, as the dog had perceived all along. Collins' detective dog belongs on the opposite side of animal imagery from what we met in the previous chapter, the hunt in a forest that begins to enclose the hunter in a dream world, and where there is often, as in the story of Actaeon, an identification of hunter and victim. The clearest example of a direct contrast to this theme is the foxhunt, where a band of red-coated sportsmen ride across open country, in late fall after the crops are reaped, in pursuit of the animal whom Jorrocks, the great hero of Robert Smith Surtees' foxhunting novels, calls "the thief of the world." The foxhunt from this point of view is a symbolic ritual aimed at the discovery of the demonic, and the fox is never killed by the hunter but is torn to pieces by the hounds, an Actaeon in reverse. Yet the fox is also the wily and resourceful hero of the beast epics who wriggles out of one tight corner after another, symbolically identical with the guileful Ulysses and his picaresque descendants.

The total social context of this is a little difficult to grasp, even though Surtees is remarkably incisive about it. The foxhunt is carried on by a horse-riding aristocracy of "barbarians," in Matthew Arnold's phrase, dominating a countryside of farmers. Jorrocks, a London Cockney merchant, is a convert to their cause, and the incongruity of his class origin and his hobby is the main source of Surtees' humor. At the end of *Handley Cross*, one of the best of these stories, Jorrocks is put on trial for his sanity. The prosecutor keeps referring to foxhunts as fetes or festivals, and to Jorrocks as a lord of misrule. He speaks in the spirit of nineteenth-century realism, and for a middleclass revolutionary movement in which the aristocracy's privileges are steadily being curtailed by a mercantile ethos which symbolizes something of the calculating wariness of a fox *redivivus*. To Jorrocks, of course, his society is equally perverted: the implication is that Jorrocks stands for a kind of romantic violence which may be post-bourgeois as well as pre-bourgeois. This is a point we must drop here and come back to later.

In more realistic stories, the theme of breaking and restoring the current of memory, or the kind of continuous action which is parallel to the memory, may be expressed in quieter ways. In Jane Austen's *Mansfield Park* the private theatricals set up in Sir Thomas Bertram's household constitute, in the author's eyes, a reversal of all normal social and moral standards, with only the heroine Fanny holding out against it. The hero's capitulation to this rebellion greatly weakens Fanny's resistance, and Fanny also finally surrenders, a sentence or two before the return of Sir Thomas puts a dramatic end both to the theatricals and to Part One. A few pages later Fanny, in a speech of a type unprecedented in Jane Austen, is uttering a eulogy on the noble faculty of the memory.

With the restoration of memory, and the continuity of action that goes with it, we have reached, so to speak, the surface of the earth, and are well on the way toward the higher themes of ascent, which take us toward the recovery of original identity. This is suggested whenever a talisman of recognition also restores the memory of the crucial character. One of the most complete and haunting examples of such a progression is the ring in the Indian play *Sakuntala*. The ring is given to Sakuntala, the heroine, by King Dushyanta, who has fallen in love with her. A curse is put on the king which makes him forget all about Sakuntala and his life with her, and in the meantime Sakuntala loses her ring. The ring falls into the sea; a fish swallows it, a fisherman catches the fish, takes it to the palace, where it is opened and the ring discovered; the ring is brought to the king's attention, and as soon as he sees it his memory is restored. Here all the elements of a total cycle of recognition are present: the descent into the lower world, the fish as a denizen of that world, the ring, symbolizing the current of memory, disappearing and returning, the period of its return being the signal for reunion.

We noted that the lower world may be submarine as well as subterranean: the sea is particularly the image of an unconscious which seems paradoxically to forget everything and yet potentially to remember everything. In any case similar complexes of objects fallen into the sea and recovered, of fish and fishermen, of the whole sense of a past life restored, inhabit a variety of comedies and romances, including *Pericles*. The biblical myth has parallels in the Jonah story and in the elaborate fishing imagery of the Gospels, where the descent of Christ to a lower world is given a submarine dimension as he and his disciples become "fishers of men." The same theme may be treated ironically, as it is in Herodotus' story of the ring of Polycrates, which that king threw into the sea to try to put a check on his good luck, but was swallowed by a fish and came back to him, indicating that the gods were still determined to be jealous of him.

In stories about the birth of a hero, a frequent opening theme is that of putting him into a chest or ark which is sent floating on the water. In one of the Gesta Romanorum stories this happens to an infant born of a union of brother and sister. The brother is killed in battle; the sister, a princess, rejects a more powerful suitor and is dispossessed from her kingdom, reduced to a single castle. The infant is rescued from the water by fishermen, and grows up in an abbey, where, on discovering the secret of his birth, he decides to become a crusader, the normal remedy for neurosis in medieval romance. His ship is driven by a storm to his mother's castle; he lands, defeats the usurper, and marries his mother. After the discovery of the second incest, another fisherman takes him to an isolated rock, from which he can only be released (this part is not clear in detail) by keys, which he throws into the sea. The keys are swallowed by a fish and extracted by a search party who are following a divine directive to make the hero the next pope. This story, which might be called the apotheosis of Oedipus, and is the basis of Thomas Mann's *The Holy Sinner*, follows logically the descent-and-return sequence in the submarine tonality.

So far the themes of romance have also been those of comedy, but now we are at a point where comedy and romance begin to diverge. We notice that utopias or ideal communities have a very restricted role in literature. Even in Plato the real form of the community is ultimately not the Republic, but the symposium of free speech and thought which contains it. The festive societies which appear at the ends of comedies are usually anti-utopian, based on the kind of pragmatic common sense or good will that transcends all social planning. But even so the theme of comedy remains predominantly social. In literature, however, the pastoral, the Arcadia, the simplified life of a handful of shepherds who are also lovers and poets, seems to represent something that carries us into a higher state of identity than the social and comic world does. The closer romance comes to a world of original identity, the more clearly something of the symbolism of the garden of Eden reappears, with the social setting reduced to the love of individual men and women within an order of nature which has been reconciled to humanity.

In *As You Like It* the melancholy Jaques is a character who feels some affinity with the jester Touchstone. Like

Touchstone, he is a kind of Brechtian alienation figure, and even tries to be a jester himself; like Touchstone, he makes a set speech turning on the number seven; and, as with Touchstone, there is no trace of him in Shakespeare's main source. At the end of the play he withdraws from the eight happily marrying characters to consult with a hermit and live in a cave. *As You Like It* is more comedy than romance: our sympathies remain with the festive group, and Jaques' withdrawal is puzzling, even ridiculous. But we have no time to wonder about him, because Rosalind comes out to speak the epilogue and ask for our applause. In *The Tempest*, which is more romance than comedy, Prospero speaks the epilogue and again asks for our applause, but the reason for the applause is to set him free for a more meditative life.

This does not mean that the world of recovered identity in romance is always a world "annihilated," in Marvell's term, to a single individual: that is merely the penseroso conclusion that leaves us with the figure of the hermit. Romance has its own conception of an ideal society, but that society is in a higher world than that of ordinary experience. We remember the two great structural principles of narrative: the polarizing and separating of a world above and a world below, and the movement through the cycles of nature and human life. We use cyclical images of spring and youth and dawn to symbolize the idyllic world, and those of winter and night and death for the lower world, but they are symbols pointing beyond themselves, and there is a considerable difference, in romance and elsewhere, between a polarization which transcends the cycle of nature and a polarization which accommodates itself to it. Thus in Christianity, although resurrection, a movement upward to a higher world, is in a sense the opposite of rebirth, we celebrate it in the images of the fertility cycle, including eggs and rabbits.

D. H. Lawrence's *The Man Who Died* is an account of the Resurrection in which Christianity, with its artificial creation myth and its hero who is the son of a sky-father, has been absorbed into a mythological universe centered on an earth-mother and perpetual renewal. The risen Christ becomes the lover of a priestess of Isis who has been taught to "wait for the reborn man," and at the end of the story he leaves her, promising to return when the cycle comes round again. Two things are notable here. One is that a female-centered mythology is likely to be even more male-dominated than its rival: when the female is at the center, the male is a comet passing her who may or may not, at his pleasure, go into a revolving orbit. The vagrant or casual wanderer, the bee pollinating the flower who could just as well have been another bee, is a central rebirth image. The other is that there is a considerable ironic element in any polarizing situation assimilated to cyclical movement, as we realize in early January when our New Year's resolutions have collapsed into habitual routine. A closer association of romance, irony, cycle, and the casual wanderer is in Joseph Conrad's *Chance*. The two parts into which this story is divided, "Damsel" and "Knight," suggest a parody of romance, and we find the damsel's life polarized between a regressive father, who is jealousy incarnate, and a lover who is generosity incarnate, which is nearly as hard on her. At the end, with father and lover dead, the character whose central place in the story was the result of sheer "chance" marries her.

Romance, in any case, eventually takes us into the great Eros theme in which a lover is driven by his love to ascend to a higher world. This ascent is full of images of climbing or flying, of mountains, towers, ladders, spiral staircases, the shooting of arrows, or coming out of the sea on to an island. The great exemplar of the theme is Dante's *Purgatorio*, where Dante is inspired by his love of Beatrice to climb a mountain leading to the Garden of Eden. In making this climb Dante is returning to his own original state as a child of Adam. This means that he is moving toward a self-recognition scene. That is, he finds and becomes his real self as it would have been if Adam had not fallen and man's original identity had been preserved. This movement upward toward self-recognition is central to romance, and is in fact what all recognition scenes really point to; but it is seldom treated so explicitly. T. S. Eliot, a devoted student of Dante, is fascinated by the theme: perhaps his most eloquent treatment of it is in the poem "Marina," a mixture of motifs from the *Purgatorio* and *Pericles*, the motto to which, beginning "Quis hic locus?" —"What place is this?"—has given me my title. Self-recognition, or attaining one's original identity, reverses all the Narcissus and twin and doppelganger themes that occur in the descent.

When Dante reaches Eden on top of the mountain, he meets a young girl named Matilda, but is separated from her by a river. Here the theme of virginity appears in another context, where it is associated with the magical preservation of the idyllic world. This association appears as late as William Morris' *The Wood Beyond the World*, where the marriage of the heroine dissolves the magical world: "all wizardry left her since the day of her wedding." In *The Tempest*, as soon as Miranda is ready to marry Ferdinand and descend into her brave new world, the magical connection between man and nature is broken, and Ariel is released. Prospero's fussing over preserving Miranda's virginity to the last moment is not morality but magic. Here again we see that there are two forms of the upward quest, one a sublimated quest ending in virginity, the other a sexual quest ending in marriage. The former usually focuses on a sister or daughter figure, as in the fourteenth-century

Pearl and any number of similar visions down to "Marina." The traditional symbolic basis of the sexual quest, which goes back to the Song of Songs in the Bible, is the identification of the mistress' body with the paradisal garden. The great medieval quest of sexual union, paralleling the sublimated quest of the *Purgatorio*, is *The Romaunt of the Rose*, where the garden modulates to a tower.

Apart from the idealizing of the pre-sexual state, there is a sense in which virginity is an appropriate image for attaining original identity: what is objectively untouched symbolizes what is subjectively contained, so to speak. More important is the sense of virginity perpetually renewed, or life in a world where every experience is fresh and unique, with the sun reborn every day, in the image of Dylan Thomas' "Fern Hill." In such a world the primary categories of experience, time and space, begin to lose the large amount of alienation they have in our experience. Time becomes less an image of fatality and destruction, and becomes rather an expression of energy, exuberance, and the kind of genuine freedom which is the same thing as discipline. The traditional symbol for this experience of time is the dance, and the original identity of the order of nature is often presented in literature as a dance. One of the most attractive of such presentations in English literature is Sir John Davies' *Orchestra*, which is of particular interest to us here because it takes us back again to the figure of the chaste Penelope. The poem is a love song sung to Penelope by the chief of her suitors, Antinous, and at the end Penelope sees in the dance of the elements of nature an image of the same kind as that of her own web, though a fuller image because it involves her feet and not merely her hands. The implication is that Penelope's weaving and unweaving is an image of the order of nature, as it must be so long as its real master remains absent from it.

Similarly, space is a world of an alienated "out there" in ordinary experience, but in the middle of it is a tiny "here," which we possess and call our home. In the upper world the Garden of Eden suggests a life in which nature itself has become home, its animals and plants a rejoined part of our society.

But, of course, in the world of Eros we can also have tragedy or frustration, of the kind expressed in all the poems deploring the cruelty of a mistress. The disdainful mistress is, in this phase at least, the incarnation of Robert Graves' white goddess or triple will, the Diana of heaven, earth, and hell whose virginity means only the elusiveness of a nature that remains unreconciled to man. As we contemplate this Diana, the symbol of nature as a closed cycle that man is trapped in, she turns into Venus flanked by her lover Mars and her child Cupid, the presiding deity of the red and white world of sexual love, the hungry desire satisfied only by death, the Eros fulfilled in Thanatos. This is the world of *The Knight's Tale* in Chaucer, where Theseus builds an amphitheater of altars to Mars, Diana, and Venus, where Arcite fights in red under Mars and Palamon in white under Venus. The red Arcite wins the battle but dies, the spilled-blood sacrifice for the marriage of Palamon and Emily.

Here again the tragic or frustrated is seen as an incomplete form of the total picture. The love for a mistress who does not need or much want such love, where the lover gives everything and the mistress gives only by a rare acceptance of a gift, is a childlike and emotionally dependent relationship which, if it is not to end in frustration, must develop into something else. The development is illustrated in the lovely story of Cupid and Psyche that floats like a soap-bubble up from Apuleius' tale of Lucius transformed to an ass. Psyche, the soul who is the bride of an invisible Love, falls under the wrath of Venus, who takes toward her the role of the conventional cruel or bullying stepmother of ballad and folktale, the latter being, as Blake's *Mental Traveller* indicates, an image of the hostility of nature in our world. Psyche is assigned impossible tasks, one of them including a journey to the world of the dead. The tasks are accomplished by spirits of nature, so that her final reconciliation with Venus is also a reconciliation of nature with the human soul, as again in the biblical theme of the regaining of Eden.

We remember that a central image of descent was that of being involved with pictures or tapestries or statues or mirrors in a way that suggested the exchange of original identity for its shadow or reflection. On the opposite side we have statues coming to life, as in the concluding scene of *The Winter's Tale;* we have stories of snow maidens thawed out and sleeping beauties awakened. The familiar Classical version is the story of Pygmalion, which is appropriately slipped in near the end of *The Romaunt of the Rose.* One very significant image of this type is the conclusion of a masque, where, as in *Comus,* the actors come out of their dramatic frame and revert to the people they actually are.

We saw that *Alice in Wonderland,* for all its lightness and humor, preserved some of the traditional imagery of a lowerworld descent. Alice passing through the looking-glass into a reversed world of dream language is also going through a descent; the incidents are largely suggested by nursery rhymes, but we may note the twin theme in Tweedledum and Tweedledee. Before long however we realize that the journey is turning upwards, in a direction symbolized by the eighth square of a chessboard, where Alice becomes a Psyche figure, a virginal queen flanked by two older queens, one red and one white, who bully her and set her impossible tasks in the form of nonsensical questions. Cards and dice, we said, have a natural connection with themes of descent into a world of fatality; chess and other board games, despite *The Waste Land*, appear more frequently in romance and in Eros contexts, as *The Tempest* again reminds us. As Alice begins to move upward out of her submarine mirror world she notes that all the poems she had heard have to do with fish, and as she wakes she reviews the metamorphoses that the figures around her had turned into.

There is no biblical counterpart to the Psyche story in Apuleius, but there is a series of apocryphal writings, of Gnostic or Manichean origin, which include "acts" of various apostles, where Philip, Thomas, John, and others go through the world performing miracles and breaking up marriages. The miracles are easy enough: their real triumphs come when they have persuaded someone of prominent social position to live apart from his wife, on the Manichean principle that humanity can only be saved by self-extermination. Suddenly, in the middle of these dreary anxieties, there comes a great trumpet call from a very different imaginative world, the "Hymn of the Soul" in the Acts of Thomas.

The Soul says that when he was a child in the palace of his father, his parents provided him with money and jewels and sent him down to Egypt, where he was to find a pearl in the sea guarded by a serpent, and come back to his original state again. He also has a brother who remained in the upper world. The Soul disguises himself and descends, but his disguise is penetrated and he is persuaded to eat the food of the lower world, like Proserpine before him. This causes him to forget both his origin and his mission, and fall into a deep sleep. His parents send a "letter" to him, the lowerworld oracle that we have met before; the Soul reads it, and as he reads his memory comes back. He puts the serpent to sleep, seizes the pearl, and starts back again. At the beginning of his quest he had been clothed in a garment which is clearly the form of his original identity. He meets this garment again and realizes that it is, in fact, his real self. He sees it "as it had been in a mirror," and it is brought him by twins: "Two, yet one shape was upon both." Putting it on, he makes his way back to his own world. Like Apuleius' story, this is a story of the "Soul"; in other words it is the story of ourselves. Crucial to it is the role of the letter or message, which not only awakens him but is what draws him upward to his self-recognition. It seems that one becomes the ultimate hero of the great quest of man, not so much by virtue of what one does, as by virtue of what and how one reads.

In traditional romance, including Dante, the upward journey is the journey of a creature returning to its creator. In most modern writers, from Blake on, it is the creative power in man that is returning to its original awareness. The secular scripture tells us that we are the creators; other scriptures tell us that we are actors in a drama of divine creation and redemption. Even Alice is troubled by the thought that her dream may not have been hers but the Red King's. Identity and self-recognition begin when we realize that this is not an either-or question, when the great twins of divine creation and human recreation have merged into one, and we can see that the same shape is upon both.

6

The Recovery of Myth

One very obvious feature of romance is its pervasive social snobbery. Naive romance confines itself largely to royal families; sentimental romance gives us patterns of aristocratic courage and courtesy, and much of it adopts a "blood will tell" convention, the association of moral virtue and social rank implied in the word "noble." A hero may appear to be of low social origin, but if he is a real hero he is likely to be revealed at the end of the story as belonging to the gentry. Even in Shakespearean romance distinctions of rank are rigidly maintained at the end. Bourgeois heroes tend to be on the industrious-apprentice model, shown in its most primitive form in the boys who arrive at the last pages of Horatio Alger working for five dollars a week with a good chance of a raise. Detective stories often feature an elegant upperclass amateur who is ever so much smarter than the merely professional police; the movies and fiction magazines of two generations ago dealt a good deal with the fabulously rich, the sex novels of our day with lovers capable of prodigies of synchronized orgasm. Here again genuine realism finds its function in parody, as, for instance, *The Great Gatsby* parodies the "success story," the romantic convention contemporary with it.

We all know, or feel that we know, why romance does this kind of thing: the reader is expected to "identify with" at least the idealized characters. And we all know, too, that this identifying process is something to be outgrown: sooner or later we recognize something immature in it. For poets and critics this is not much of a danger, but what most of them have to pass through, at some time and in some form, is identification with an author, usually as an intense form of discipleship. We often find in literature metaphors suggesting a kind of poetic reincarnation, such as Blake employs about Milton or Spenser about Chaucer, when Spenser speaks of "Thine own spirit, which doth in me survive." Sometimes, as with Chaucer's "Lollius," the master may be purely fictional, a symbol of the literary tradition. Middleton Murry saw Keats as struggling between a good and an evil angel of identification, one named Shakespeare and the other Milton. When Keats wrote "To Autumn," says Murry, Shakespeare had triumphed in Keats's soul, because "To Autumn" is such a good poem.

This attitude has recently revived as a form of existential criticism. Its method is brilliantly satirized in Borges' story of Pierre Menard, whose life's work it was to rewrite a couple of chapters of *Don Quixote*, not by copying them, but by total identification with Cervantes. Borges quotes a passage from Cervantes and a passage from Menard which is identical with it to the letter, and urges us to see how much more historical resonance there is in the Menard copy. The satire shows us clearly that nothing will get around the fact that writer and reader are different entities in time and space, that whenever we read anything, even a letter from a friend, we are translating it into something else. Dante tells us that he could never have got through hell and purgatory without the instruction of Virgil. Virgil, many centuries later, when interviewed by Anatole France in Elysium, complained that Dante had totally misunderstood him. Without going in quite the same direction that some critics have done, I think it is true that this is how the recreating of the literary tradition often has to proceed: through a process of absorption followed by misunderstanding, that is, establishing a new context. Thus an alleged misunderstanding of Ovid produced a major development in medieval poetry, and some later romance is bound up with such phrases as "Gothic revival" and "Celtic twilight," misunderstandings of earlier ages that never existed.

But if romance so often appears as a kind of naive social snobbery, what becomes of the revolutionary quality in it that we mentioned earlier, the proletarian element rejected by every cultural establishment? We remember that we found the focus of this revolutionary quality near the end of a romantic story, usually at the recognition scene. It appears in the polarizing between two worlds, one desirable and the other hateful, the triumphant upward movement of the living hero rising from the dead dragon, the point that expresses the reader's identity with a power of life strong enough to smash through any kind of barrier or danger. In Christianity the archetype of the completed romance is Christ rising from the dragon of death and hell with his redeemed captives; but the central figure need not take on such portentous overtones. The heroine who is saved from rape or sacrifice, even if she merely avoids Mr. Wrong and marries Mr. Right, is reenacting the ancient ritual which in Greek religion is called the anabasis of Kore, the rising of a maiden, Psyche or Cinderella or Richardson's Pamela or Aristophanes' Peace, from a lower to a higher world.

Spenser, though speaking for an establishment, understood this very well, and in the first book of *The Faerie Queene* he described the victory of the Protestant revolution in England under the ancient myth of St. George killing his dragon. The Waverley novels were written by a Tory, yet the defeated insurgent forces, the Jacobite Highlanders in *Waverley*, the supporters of Queen Mary in *The Abbot*, the Saxons in *Ivanhoe*, express the greatest social passion and power in those novels. The fact that Scott was a Tory is connected with his being also a historical novelist. The struggles he describes are within the cycle of history, and never suggest any ultimate transcending of history. In this respect he is a contrast with William Morris, who raises the opposite problem. How, we wonder, could a writer who was a radical socialist, very politically involved with revolutionary activities, spend so much of his time writing what often seem like very self-indulgent romances? The same question was asked, much less sympathetically, by Morris' anarchist comrades, who eventually forced him out of the party. Their attitude foreshadowed a very similar issue which appeared in the Soviet Union during the Stalin regime in the thirties.

There is a strongly conservative element at the core of realism, an acceptance of society in its present structure, an attitude of mind that helps to make Balzac typical of realism, just as the opposite revolutionary attitude helps to make Victor Hugo typical of romanticism. The Stalinist bureaucracy adopted a doctrine of "social realism" as part of the authoritarian aspect of its rule, rationalized by the dogma that romanticism is a form of bourgeois ideology, and that Marxism represents the only possible combination of the revolutionary with the realistic. The essential idea of this version of "social realism" was protest before revolution, panegyric afterward. Genuine realism, in certain contexts, does have a revolutionary social function:

this function consists mainly in opposing, by parody, the kidnapping of romance, and of literature and culture in general, by an ascendant class. Napoleon patronized such painters as David, but it is Goya's Disasters of War that tell the truth about the kind of thing that Napoleon is and does in the world. According to the Stalinist scheme, writers outside the Soviet Union would follow this tradition of realism: writers inside it would set up a new kind of kidnapped romanticism, celebrating the glories of the de facto power, slightly disguised by harmless criticism and by talk about a continuing process of building socialism. Maxim Gorky gave his support to this program, though it was Gorky, in an earlier and more genuinely creative period, who clearly saw the real link between the revolutionary and the romantic. It is possible that social, political, or religious revolution always, and necessarily, betrays a revolutionary ideal of which the imagination alone preserves the secret.

Similar phenomena may be observed in our own culture. The soap operas of radio and television are addressed primarily to a female audience, and feature a heroine plunged into the woes typical of so many forms of romance. But while she continually struggles against a swarm of complications, the decisive polarizing of romance does not take place. She never quite reaches what I have been calling the night world, a life so intolerable that it must end either in tragedy or in a permanent escape. This is partly so that the story, along with the financial support of its sponsors, can last indefinitely, but there is another social dimension involved.

In speaking of figures of identification I mixed up two general types. Both are in a larger sense romantic; but the princes and knights of naive romance are romantic in a way that bourgeois heroes and industrious apprentices are not. These latter are presented under a guise of realism, often as models we could conceivably follow. The models sometimes have real-life prototypes, such as Benjamin Franklin; consequently some sense of society must appear in the background, however simplified. Similarly with the soap operas just mentioned, which in some isolated areas, like Newfoundland outports, are eagerly discussed in detail over party-line telephones whenever a new installment comes out. What is identified with here is the society being portrayed in the story, to the extent that a society is present, and such identification is a sign of a fairly thoroughgoing conservatism.

This brings us to the problem of criticism represented by Don Quixote at the puppet show or Huckleberry Finn at the circus or small children with a department-store Santa Claus. What the naive, uninstructed, childlike or illusion-ridden viewer accepts as "real" a more knowledgeable and emancipated one sees to be a carefully planned show, and planned within the framework of a literary convention. It follows that the journey toward one's own identity, which literature does so much to help with, has a great deal to do with escaping from the alleged "reality" of what one is reading or looking at, and recognizing the convention behind it. The same process exists in the elementary teaching of literature, or should. The child should not "believe" the story he is told; he should not disbelieve it either, but send out imaginative roots into that mysterious world between the "is" and the "is not" which is where his own ultimate freedom lies.

Society, we said, makes a special and nonliterary use of myth, which causes it to form a mythology and eventually a mythological universe. Such a mythology surrounds us on all sides, and on several levels. The lowest level is that of the cliché mythology that soaks into us from early childhood, from parents, teachers, classmates, news media, popular culture, and the judicious mixture of flattery and threats in advertising. On this level social mythology is adjustment mythology, designed to produce the docile and obedient citizen. It "indoctrinates," as we say, not because anyone, at least in our society, wants it to or plans it that way, but because the whole enterprise is automatic and mindless, an expression not of social unity but of gregariousness. Professional educators, in North America at least, appear to be dedicated to the proposition that school children should learn as much as possible of this adjustment mythology, and as little as possible of anything else. The demand for "relevance" is a hoarse echo of the same axiom.

Every teacher of literature should realize that literary experience is only the visible tip of the verbal iceberg: below it is a subliminal area of rhetorical response, addressed by advertising, social assumptions, and casual conversation, that literature as such, on however popular a level of movie or television or comic book, can hardly reach. What confronts the teacher of literature is the student's whole verbal experience, including this subliterary nine-tenths of it. One of the things that the study of literature should do is to help the student become aware of his own mythological conditioning, especially on the more passive and critically unexamined levels. It is, of course, unlikely to do this as long as the teachers are unconscious victims of the same conditioning.

Popular romance, in whatever media it may come, is often an expression of a frivolous or silly social mythology, and a value judgment on the social mythology is likely to be more relevant to criticism than a value judgment on the literary merit. This principle increases in importance when the mythology is not merely silly but actively vicious or evil. Take the following passage from a story in O. Henry's *The Gentle Grafter:*

"Two months ago," says Buckingham Skinner, "I was doing well down in Texas with a patent instantaneous fire kindler, made of compressed wood ashes and benzine. I sold loads of 'em in towns where they like to burn niggers quick, without having to ask somebody for a light. And just when I was doing the best they strikes oil down there and puts me out of business. 'Your machine's too slow, now, pardner,' they tells me. 'We can have a coon in hell with this here petroleum before your old flint-and-tinder truck can get him warm enough to perfess religion.' "

[the narrator comments] I liked Buckingham Skinner from the start, for as good a man as ever stood over the axles and breathed gasoline smoke.

This passage will illustrate, first, what such a word as "obscene" really means, and, second, that real obscenity is not neutralized by a serious literary intention, as is assumed in the futile anxieties of censorship, but is a quality of the social mythology that the writer accepts.

What we have called kidnapped romance is usually romance that expresses a social mythology of this more uncritical kind, which may be intense but is not deep, and is founded on prejudice and unexamined assumptions. R. M. Ballantyne's *The Coral Island*, a story for boys written in the nineteenth century, features three English lads who have been shipwrecked on a South Sea island. They live a happy life there for some months, but when "natives" turn up they show that they belong to an officer caste as well. It is common knowledge that William Golding's *Lord of the Flies* is in part a parody of *The Coral Island*. But it is significant that *Lord of the Flies*, appearing after the decline of realism, is not strictly a realistic parody. It uses the same paradisal archetype as its predecessor, but develops it in a more comprehensive way, bringing out the corruption of human nature that has always been an essential part of the archetype. *The Coral Island* is by no means a stupid book, but it is, to use Robert Frost's image about realism, a somewhat over-scrubbed potato: the effect of all that clean living is to produce a superficial reflex response, like the gleaming smiles of a toothpaste ad.

Rider Haggard remarked that a series of adventures was easy enough to write, but that a real story had to have a "heart," that is, a focus or center implying a total shape with a beginning and an end. The series of adventures that he said was easy appears in the more rudimentary forms of romance represented by continuous comic strips and the interminable radio and television serials just mentioned. These in turn have a long tradition, much older than the "vast French romances" of *The Rape of the Lock*, of stories in which we seldom get a clear sight of progress toward a conclusion. Such stories do not end: they stop, and very frequently they can be easily started again. They are designed to provide a kind of idealized shadow of the continuum of our lives, an endless dream world in which we can keep losing ourselves.

A modulation of the endless romance is the linking together of a series of stories by a frame providing a unified setting. The root of this in human life is, possibly, the child's bedtime story: the Arabian Nights setting also preserves the sense of a threshold to a dream world. *The Canterbury Tales*, *The Faerie Queene*, Dickens' *Master Humphrey's Clock*, and Morris' *Earthly Paradise* are examples showing how powerful the impulse is to derive a sequence of romances from a setting providing some unity of place. This unity of place has been technologically achieved by the television tube, which provides, at least in centers where there is a round-the-clock supply of programs, a shadow counterpart for the whole continuum of existence, dreaming as well as waking. The impact of television had a good deal to do with the drug cults and social hysteria of the late sixties, which showed symptoms both of a withdrawal from waking reality and of an irritability of the sort produced by dream deprivation. More important, it made the impact of cliché mythology so intolerable that it provoked a frenzied rejection of it, followed, as such outbreaks must be, by a kind of stupor.

Unconsciously acquired social mythology, the mythology of prejudice and conditioning, is clearly also something to be outgrown: it is therapeutic to recognize and reject it, as with other repressed material. Lying beyond it is the next level of social mythology, or, roughly speaking, the area of serious belief. A belief, in this sense, is essentially a statement of a desire to attach oneself to, or live in or among, a specific kind of community. America has a genuine social mythology in which beliefs in personal liberty, democracy, and equality before law have a central place. Every major American writer will be found to have struck his roots deeply into this serious social mythology, even if he advocates civil disobedience or makes speeches in a country with which America is at war. Genuine social mythology, whether religious or secular, is also to be transcended, but transcendence here does not mean repudiating or getting rid of it, except in special cases. It means rather an individual recreation of the mythology, a transforming of it from accepted social values into the axioms of one's own activity.

The traditional attitude of society is that its concern must always be primary, and that all individual action should move within its orbit. In historical Christianity, as in Marxism today, an intense indoctrinating process begins in childhood: the individual may be allowed to rediscover and recreate these doctrines, but without altering them to a degree that would alarm social concern. A conservative, mystical strain of social or religious acceptance runs all through romance, from the Grail stories of the Middle Ages through Novalis and George MacDonald in the nineteenth century to C. S. Lewis and Charles Williams a generation ago. For the poet, an intense commitment to certain beliefs is often a necessity: we see this particularly in religious belief, which to so many poets of the last century seemed the only possible basis on which the creative imagination could operate. But of course when beliefs are presented within literature, the impact on the reader is purely imaginative, and it is unnecessary for him to share or even sympathize with those beliefs to respond appropriately. Imaginative response transcends belief of all kinds, and this takes us back to the divergence of romance from comedy that I mentioned in the previous chapter.

Comedy ends with a festive society: it is contained by social assumptions. Belief, I am saying, is essentially a form of attachment to a community: in other words belief is also primarily social in reference, which is why the Christian myth is a comedy rather than a romance. Virgil leaves Dante at the summit of Purgatory, crowning and mitering him, making him Pope and Emperor over himself, as a man who has attained free will. Then a stern and scolding Beatrice appears, Dante is reduced to a whimpering and tearful child, and the comic-providential universe closes around us again as Dante prepares to enter the City of God. But for one instant we have had a glimpse of the secular scripture, of what Wallace Stevens means when he says that the great poems of heaven and hell have been written but the great poem of earth has still to be written.

All societies, including the City of God, are free only to the extent that they arrange the conditions of freedom for the individual, because the individual alone can experience freedom. This principle is, of course, as true of democracy and Marxism as it is of Christianity.

Romance has no continuing city as its final resting place. In folktales and fairy tales the chief characters live in a kind of atomized society: there is only the most shadowy sense of a community, and their kings and princesses are individuals given the maximum of leisure, privacy, and freedom of action. In real life, of course, royal figures have even less of such things than other people: it is different in stories. The same disintegrated society reappears in the cells of hermits, the caves of ogres, the cottages hidden in forests; in the shepherds of pastoral, the knights errant who wander far from courts and castles, the nomadic ranchers and rustlers of Western stories, which are a later form of pastoral, and their descendants in the easy-riding school founded by Jack Kerouac. The Bible is a divine comedy, with society gathered into one body at the end; the secular scripture is a human romance, and its ideals seem to be different.

These ideals, we saw, are commonly symbolized by some kind of paradise or park like the biblical Eden, a world in which a humanity greatly reduced in numbers has become reconciled to nature. Such an ideal represents an attitude to nature which is the opposite of that of the cycle of violence and cunning that begins with Homer. In this cycle man is enclosed within nature, nature being something that renews but inexorably destroys again, and seems to be controlled by mysterious and capricious gods. This vision has revived in Yeats and in Robert Graves, the latter telling his son Juan that in a woman's world dominated by the white goddess of nature, man can only keep warm in December by remembering what it was like in June. But in our day we have passed through and inherited the biblical view that there are no gods or numinous forces in nature, and that man has to find the clues to his destiny within his own institutions. The dragon-killing and giant-quelling of chivalric romance suggests a civilizing force gradually increasing its control of a turbulent natural order. The myth of Eden, similarly, suggests a final reconciliation with nature as something to be attained after the human community has been reordered. We reach the ideal of romance through a progressive bursting of closed circles, first of social mythology, whether frivolous or serious, then of nature, and finally of the comic-providential universe of Christianity and other religions, including Marxism, which contains them both.

Revolutionary social ideals are traditionally those of liberty, equality, and fraternity, and the first two seem to be particularly the concern of comedy, whose tendency it is to gather all its characters together in the final scene and assign certain rights and functions to each one. After exhausting these images, romance's last vision seems to be that of fraternity, Kant's kingdom of ends where, as in fairy tales, we are all kings and princesses. The principle of the aristocracies of the past was respect for birth; the principle of fraternity in the ideal world of romance is respect rather for those who have been born, and because they have been born.

We have been using the word "cycle" to describe the total story of romance, and the simplest form of a story with Rider Haggard's "heart" or quest in it is the closed-circle or *nostos* form of the *Odyssey*, where Ulysses, after massacring the suitors and hanging the servant maids, climbs back into bed with Penelope—the point at which, according to tradition, the *Odyssey* originally ended. The emotional overtones of such a closed circle may be ironic, suggesting that there is nothing worth doing that does not have to be done over again, as in E. R. Eddison's story *The Worm Ouroboros*. Sometimes, however, the irony is only half the story, and the cycle in that case becomes the only possible way of suggesting what is beyond the cycle. This is what Eliot's "East Coker" is saying in its circular motto, "In my beginning is my end"; it is what Camus means when he says that we have to think of Sisyphus as a happy man, and it may be what *Finnegans Wake* is saying on its final page, in such phrases as "Till thousends thee," just before we swing back to the beginning again. *Ulysses* concludes with the monologue of Molly Bloom, who seems a pure white-goddess figure, the incarnation of a cyclical nature who embraces and abandons one lover after another. And yet she too is an embodiment of the chaste Penelope, and at the end of her ruminations she goes back to something very like the dawn of a first love.

More frequently, the quest romance takes on a spiral form, an open circle where the end is the beginning transformed and renewed by the heroic quest. Dante's *Inferno* is a descending spiral, taking us into narrowing and unchangeable closed circles; the *Purgatorio* spiral gives us the opposite creative movement. When Dante reaches the presence of God at the end of the *Paradiso*, the universe turns inside out, becoming God-centered instead of earth-centered, an end that reverses the beginning of all things. Dante is within the orbit of the sacred scripture, where God is the creator, but the same principle of reversed movement can be associated with human creativity. Such a reversal occurs at the end of Proust, where an experience of repetition transforms Marcel's memory of his life into a potential imaginative vision, so that the narrator comes to the beginning of his book at the point where the reader comes to the end of it. Time being irreversible, a return to a starting point, even in a theory of recurrence as naive as Nietzsche's, can only be a symbol for something else. The past is not returned to; it is recreated, and when time in Proust is found again (*retrouvé*), the return to the beginning is a metaphor for creative repetition.

Creative repetition is of course one of the central principles of all criticism, which has held for many centuries that poetry presents a kind of controlled hallucination: something in the past, normally accessible only to the memory, is brought into the present by the imagination. Hence, as Hobbes explains, the Greek tradition that the mother of the muses is Mnemosyne, memory. This conception of the creative function of memory is violently attacked by William Blake, who insists that "imagination has nothing to do with memory," and yet Blake is really expounding a different aspect of the same principle. For Blake the imagination brings to life the specters of the dead, as he calls them, who inhabit the memory, creation thus being to memory what resurrection is to death. The notion of a world of pure memory, where everything forever continues to be as it has been, is the core of the religious conception of hell, which is why Blake dislikes it. But of course nobody's memory is like this: all memory is selective, and the fact that it is selective is the starting point of creation. Plato's doctrine of *anamnesis* or recollection, that we can know only what we *re*-cognize or re-experience, is a projection of the fact that a memory can be objectified in a conscious being, hence repeated, hence recreated.

I spoke of the end of Canto 27 of the *Purgatorio*, where Virgil makes Dante his own Pope and Emperor before taking leave of him. In Yeats's "Dialogue of Self and Soul" the poet arrives at much the same place, but then splits in two. The "soul" wants to keep climbing, as Dante does, to seek ultimate forgiveness and atonement in a world still further up. The "self," representing the creative power of the poet, looks down from the top of the world into his own memory of his past life, and sees that for him there is nothing for it but to go back into the world of love and war, of suffering and humiliation, of nausea and self-contempt, so that he may finally come back up again possessing the vision of innocence and the holiness of all things with which the poem concludes. Yeats's poem is not about reincarnation, even if Yeats thought it was: it is about the fact that creation is essentially a recreating of memory. In turning away from what the "soul" thinks of as God's world, the "self" or poet in his creation is also imitating the creative activity of God. This has been a central principle of criticism at least since Elizabethan times. Mallarmé tells us that a dice-throw does not abolish chance, meaning, roughly, that human creation does not deliver us from death, though it is all that we have to fight death with. But the context of this conclusion is a work called *Igitur*, the title of which refers to the verse in Genesis about the end of the original creation: "Thus (igitur) the heavens and the earth were finished, and all the host of them."

The frequent association of romance with the historical, such as we see in the Waverley novels, is based, I should think, on the principle that there is a peculiar emotional intensity in contemplating something, including our own earlier lives, that we know we have survived. But there is beyond this a special kind of transformation of the past which is distinctive of romance. Our descending and ascending themes showed us two contrasting organizations of human life. Themes of ascent are pervaded by struggles to escape and survive: the other side, of descent and disappearing identity, takes place in a world of violent and cunning leaders. This is the world of order and degree, the world that tragedy and tragic irony present from the inside, the world celebrated in the famous speech about degree by Ulysses in *Troilus and Cressida,* Shakespeare's most ironic play.

Romance usually presents us with a hierarchical social order, and in what we have called kidnapped romance, this order is rationalized. Thus chivalric romance rationalizes the social structure of the feudal system, in which few medieval barons resembled the knights of the Round Table. Later writers of romance fall into a kind of sliding scale of projection and recovery in their attitude to the past. The projecting writers fall in love with the hierarchical structures that they find in earlier history, and present them as ideals to be recreated in their past forms. There is a good deal of this in Carlyle, with his over-simplified work ethic which leads him to a dream of a reactivated aristocracy. There is a good deal of it in Yeats, with his carpet-knight adulation of some very dubious leaders and his fatalistic "vision" of history, and a good deal of it in such writers as G. K. Chesterton who think within a mythology of decline from earlier standards of authority, and identify recreation with their revival. Here again I am not speaking of literary merit, but of the quality of social mythology accepted. In projected romance the past becomes the mirror of the future, and we remember from our survey of descent themes that remaining imprisoned within a mirror world keeps us in the basement of reality.

William Morris is an example of a writer whose attitude to the past is one of creative repetition rather than of return. Morris admired the Middle Ages to the point of fixation, and yet the social reference of his medievalism is quite different from that of Carlyle, or even Ruskin, who so strongly influenced him. According to Morris, the Middle Ages appears right side up, so to speak, when we see it as a creation of artists, not in its reflected or projected form as a hierarchy; when we realize that the genuine creators of medieval culture were the builders and painters and romancers, not the warriors or the priests. For him the fourteenth century was the time when, with the Peasants' Revolt, something like a genuine proletariat appeared on the social scene, its political attitude expressed in John Ball's question, where were the "gentlemen" in the working society of Adam and Eve? In *News from Nowhere*, the "dream of John Ball" (the title of another work of Morris) comes true: the people in that happy future world are an equal society of creative workers. They have not returned to the fourteenth century: they have turned it inside out.

As we make the first great move from projection to the recovery of myth, from return to recreation, the focus of interest shifts from heroes and other elements of narrative toward the process of creating them. The real hero becomes the poet, not the agent of force or cunning whom the poet may celebrate. In proportion as this happens, the inherently revolutionary quality in romance begins to emerge from all the nostalgia about a vanished past. Even for Yeats the same thing happens in his less occulted moments: in his early play *The King's Threshold*, for instance, where we are shown that kings would have no motivation to act like kings if poets did not provide the imaginative conception of kingship.

Don Quixote sounds like an unlikely source for such a romantic revolutionary vision, but there is one there nonetheless. The Quixote who tries to actualize in his life the romances he has been reading is a psychotic, though a psychotic of unusual literary interest. I suppose psychosis, or certain forms of it at least, could almost be defined as an attempt to identify one's life "literally" with an imaginative projection. But in the second part of the book, Sancho Panza is given an island to rule, and rules it very well:

while he is doing so, Don Quixote offers him advice which is surprisingly sensible. Earlier I quoted Borges as describing the story we are calling the secular scripture as a search for some dearly loved Mediterranean island. I suspect that Borges' island has a good deal to do with Cervantes' island, a society where Sancho Panza, who is not a Machiavellian prince but one of us, is ruler, and where Don Quixote, possibly the greatest figure in the history of romance, has recovered his proper function as a social visionary.

We are perhaps beginning to see at this point that to recreate the past and bring it into the present is only half the operation. The other half consists of bringing something into the present which is potential or possible, and in that sense belongs to the future. This recreation of the possible or future or ideal constitutes the wish-fulfillment element in romance, which is the normal containing form, as archaism or the presentation of the past is the normal content. Thus the recreation of romance brings us into a present where past and future are gathered, in Eliot's phrase. It is also Eliot who shows us that the starting point of creation is the impinging of wish-thinking on the memory, the intrusion of "it might have been" into "it was" that we encounter at the opening of "Burnt Norton." Eliot's rose garden, which is created out of this intrusion, seems very remote from Morris' vision in which the preindustrial craftsmanship of the Middle Ages provides a model for a postindustrial Arcadia, but they are symbolic first cousins for all that, Adam and Eve being their common grandparents. Such a union of past and future in a present vision of a pastoral, paradisal, and radically simplified form of life obviously takes on a new kind of urgency in an age of pollution and energy crisis, and helps to explain why romance seems so contemporary a form of literary experience.

Technology, for capitalism and still more for Communism, seemed at one time to promise the kind of human ascendancy over nature that would accompany the final recovery of myth, but the poets have dragged their feet in its celebration. Blake, D. H. Lawrence, Morris, Yeats, Pound, are only a few of those who have shown marked hostility to technology and have refused to believe that its peaceful and destructive aspects can be separated. The poets see nothing imaginative in a domination of nature which expresses no love for it, in an activity founded on will, which always overreacts, in a way of life marked by a constant increase in speed, which means also an increase in introversion and the breaking down of genuine personal relationships. The great exception, the literary movement that was expected to seize on technology as its central theme, was assumed to be science fiction. But the way in which science fiction, as it has developed from hardware fantasy into software philosophical romance, has fallen into precisely the conventions of romance as outlined here is so extraordinary that I wish I had the time and the erudition to give it a separate treatment. Visions of utopias, or properly running communities, belong in its general area; but, in modern science fiction, anti-utopias, visions of regression or the nightmarish insect states of imaginative death, must outnumber the positive utopias by at least fifty to one.

The guides who supervise tourists in developing countries, especially Marxist ones, always want to take them to the collective farms, engineering projects, and other monuments of the existing regime, and are often puzzled or annoyed when the tourists want to see the works of art that were produced in the old exploiting days. The reason for this takes us further into the theory of criticism than we might suppose. Such words as "classic" or "masterpiece" tell us nothing about the structure of literary works: they refer to social acceptance, and there are no inherent formal qualities that classics or masterpieces have that other works do not have. If there were, criticism would be a much easier occupation, if a less rewarding one. It is very different with the sense of formal design in, say, the cultural products in a museum, which may range from Benin bronzes to Viking ships, from Chinese pottery to Peruvian textiles. We know that all the cruelty and folly of which man is capable was all around these artifacts when they were produced, and that some of that cruelty and folly may be reflected from the art itself. Nevertheless there is something in the energy of design and the purity of outline that lifts them clear of all this. Whatever the culture was, its designed products belong in the state of innocence, as remote from the evils of that culture as Marina was from the brothel in *Pericles*. I have not given this example at random: Marina in the brothel represents a corresponding power of formal design in the literary arts, and is therefore, like all highly concentrated art, in one sense art talking about itself.

We started this argument with a distinction between myth and fable in which myth has priority in social importance. This in our tradition has given the Bible, as the epic of which God is the hero, the central place. We said that a sexual creation myth, which has a natural focus on an earth-mother figure, was superseded, in our tradition, by an artificial creation myth in which the world was made by a sky-father. So far as such myths condition our sense of external reality, the change seems to have been a retrograde step. It is impossible to reconcile a story of God making things in roughly their present forms with the real story of nature, where an evolution of complex organisms out of simpler ones gives a much more satisfactory vision of "genesis," however many gaps there may still be in our

knowledge. The artificial myth won out, obviously, because it made reality humanly intelligible, giving us a
world that begins and ends in time, that has a top and a
bottom in at least metaphorical space. It looks at the
moment as though these human limitations make the artificial creation myth only a projection of the fact that man
creates and makes things. But it still has a powerful grip on
the human imagination, and one wonders if there are other
factors suggesting that it may be something more than
that.

We noticed that in this myth God makes only a model
world, and that the difference between it and the world we
are in now has to be accounted for by supplying the alienation myth of a "fall" to complete the story of creation. In
the great cycle of descent and ascent that we have been
studying in romance, themes of descent are connected with
the establishing of order, authority, and hierarchy, and
the artificial creation myth is the first narrative unit of that
descent. The creation-fall is thus the starting point of the
whole complex of social acceptance, in which laws, rituals,
customs, and the authority of warriors and priests and
kings are all manifestations of the otherness of the spirit I
mentioned earlier. Everything man has that seems most
profoundly himself is thought of as coming to him from
outside, descending from the most ancient days in time,
coming down from the remotest heights in space. We belong to something before we are anything, and, just as an
infant's world has an order of parents already in it, so
man's first impulse is to project figures of authority, or
precedence in time and space, stretching in an iron chain of
command back to God.

Where we came from is the main subject of the myths
that carry the primary authority of social concern, and
play so large a part in rationalizing our acceptance of such

authority. The imagination, as it reflects on this world, sees it as a world of violence and cunning, *forza* and *froda*. The typical agent of cunning is a woman, whose main instrument of will is her bed: in the *Iliad* even the greatest of goddesses, Hera, decoys Zeus in this way in an effort to aid the Greeks. Thus the *forza-froda* cycle is also that of Ares and Eros, both of which, for human beings, end in Thanatos or death. Ares and Eros are functionaries of Venus, whose alternative form is Diana of the triple will, the white goddess who always kills, and whose rebirth is only for herself.

Romance, the kernel of fable, begins an upward journey toward man's recovery of what he projects as sacred myth. At the bottom of the mythological universe is a death and rebirth process which cares nothing for the individual; at the top is the individual's regained identity. At the bottom is a memory which can only be returned to, a closed circle of recurrence: at the top is the recreation of memory. In romance violence and sexuality are used as rocket propulsions, so to speak, in an ascending movement. Violence becomes melodrama, the separating of heroes from villains, angels of light from giants of the dark. Sexuality becomes a driving force with a great deal of sublimation in it. In the traditional romance, where the heroine is so often a virgin reaching her first sexual contact on the last page, the erotic feeling is sublimated for the action of the story. The much more thoroughgoing sublimation in our two greatest Eros poets, Plato and Dante, needs no further elaboration here.

As we go up, we find ourselves surrounded by images of increased participation: with human society, in the festive endings of comedy; with nature, in pastoral and Arcadian imagery; with aspects of divinity, in myths of redemption. The conception of evolution is an ascending metamorphosis myth of this kind, attaching us to the whole family of living things. Goethe's essays on the metamorphoses of plants link the conception of evolution to that of the secular scripture, and introduce some of the traditional ascent motifs, connecting straight-line ascent with the symbolically "male" and spiral ascent with the symbolically "female." The end of fable, as the total body of verbal imagination that man constructs, brings us back to the beginning of myth, the model world associated with divine creation in Genesis.

The model world seems to us now, however, not like a past state to return to, but an inner model or social vision to be recreated out of our "lower" world of experience, the real creative power, as we see it, being something that comes from below. What the artificial creation myth appears to be telling us is that, somehow or other, models for human creation have been implanted in the human mind. However they got there, and whoever gave them to us (and the traditional metaphors are of course expendable), in developing the forms of culture and civilization we seem to be recreating something that we did not get from nature. Whether this is true or not, the artificial creation myth still has an essential function for us: it emphasizes the uniqueness, the once-for-all quality, in the creative act, and helps to deliver us, if not from death or Mallarmé's "chance," at least from the facile ironies of an endlessly turning cycle.

In the descending hierarchical order, where the individual is primarily a unit of his society, there is a sense of growing isolation that intensifies as we reach a place in which we feel that, as Sartre says, hell is other people. The creative act is an individualizing act, hence, for all the sense of participation, we are also returning to a second kind of isolation. As Goethe also notes about the ascend-

ing metamorphosis of plants, there is a process of renun-
ciation in the ascent as well, a cutting off of everything
from the liberated individual. The cells of the hermits who
so often appear in high romance have real-life prototypes
in Thoreau's Walden retreat, and in Indian yoga, with its
conception of identity as something to be gained by sup-
pressing the metamorphoses of the mind. We have already
found expressions of this in the "penseroso" cadences of
romance: it also comes into the theme of the renounced
quest, the story for example of Shelley's Prometheus, who
becomes free as soon as he stops trying to fight the tyran-
nical Jupiter whom he has created himself, and keeps in
business by resisting. The same theme dominates the story
told by Wagner and retold by Tolkien, of a stolen ring that
has to be given back, a return that achieves its recreation
by a creatively negative act, a cancelling out of a wrong
action.

The artificial creation story in Genesis culminates in the
Sabbath vision, in which God contemplates what he has
made. In human life creation and contemplation need two
people, a poet and a reader, a creative action that produces
and a creative response that possesses. We may recall that
the Dante who achieved freedom of will at the top of Purgatory was not merely Dante the poet, but Dante the student of Virgil. The first step in the recovery of myth is the
transfer of the center of interest from hero to poet. The
second, and perhaps final, stage is reached when the poet
entrusts his work to his reader, as Joyce, after spending
seventeen years on the great dream of Finnegan, handed it
over to what he called "the ideal reader suffering from an
ideal insomnia."

Such a reader of *Finnegans Wake* clearly would need
some heroic qualities, but even with less difficult works it
is still true that there is a perspective from which the

reader, the mental traveler, is the hero of literature, or at least of what he has read. As we have seen, the message of all romance is *de te fabula:* the story is about you; and it is the reader who is responsible for the way literature functions, both socially and individually. His duty may not constitute what a once famous pious work called the whole duty of man, but there is no whole duty without it. One's reading thus becomes an essential part of a process of self-creation and self-identity that passes beyond all the attached identifications, with society or belief or nature, that we have been tracing. Such a reader, contemplating the cycle of descent into subjects and objects, where we die each other's lives, as Heraclitus says, and of ascent to identity where we live each other's deaths, is a Moses who can see the promised land, in contrast to the Joshua who merely conquers Canaan, and so begins another cycle of descent.

Moses' vision was the climax of his career as the leader of a wandering people. The normal form of romance is the quest story that reflects the cyclical movement we have been tracing; but we also found continuous or "endless" forms in various types of popular literature. There is always something of the nomadic in romance, something that recalls its heritage of traveling folktales and ballads. Recurrently, from Surtees' foxhunting stories to the biblical vision of two people in a garden that stretched from Egypt to (according to Josephus) India, we have seen romance associating itself with an imaginative uprooting, a drive over and across everything settled and planted and built. It is perhaps easiest to see this "endless" form in the great Oriental romances, such as the Japanese tale of Genji, where it is congenial to religious and other perspectives in the culture; but it is inherent in romance, and is returning in our own literature today.

In the last scene of *A Midsummer Night's Dream* that very shrewd critic Hippolyta remarks that Peter Quince's play is the silliest stuff she has ever heard. But, says Theseus, whose conception of the imagination is confused because he is preoccupied with his own "image" as a gracious prince, the worst plays are no worse than the best, "if imagination amend them." It must be your imagination, then, says Hippolyta, and not theirs. For Theseus the one thing good in Peter Quince's play is the fact that it is offered to him, and he confers merit on it by accepting it. Such an attitude would be more appropriate for God, perhaps, than a Duke of Athens, but then Theseus thinks of himself as in some degree a human representative of God. It is Hippolyta who has, however unconsciously, expressed the real goal of humanism. In the world of order and hierarchy there are literary hierarchies too, the order of "classics" and "masterpieces." Genuine humanism is not a return to this order, but an imaginative recreation of it: we admire them and do something else, as Hopkins says. Homer and Shakespeare, both of whom have minstrels and jongleurs among their characters, do not lose their importance in our experience when the wandering tribes of folktale and anecdote, of popular story and ballad and nursery rhyme, find a home there too. The mythological universe is not an ordered hierarchy but an interpenetrating world, where every unit of verbal experience is a monad reflecting all the others. This is the human counterpart of the vision symbolized in Genesis as the Sabbath vision: it is how the world looks after the ego has collapsed. The "outside" world disappears, but it does not disappear into the "inside": that kind of metaphor has been left far behind.

The greatest romance in English literature, and one of the supreme romances of the world, is Spenser's *Faerie*

Queene. The six books of this epic end with the quest of courtesy, the word of man, as the integrating force of the human community. This sixth book is full of the pastoral imagery which belongs to the higher reaches of romance; the poet himself appears near the end of it, and the enemy of courtesy, the Blatant Beast, slander or bad words, escapes again at the end. His escape suggests an ironic closed-circle containing form for the whole epic. Then, after his six efforts of creation, Spenser gives us an epilogue or Sabbath vision, in the great poem called the Mutabilitie Cantoes. At the end of this poem the poet identifies himself with God's contemplative vision of the model created world, and the last line reads: "O that great Sabbaoth God graunt me that Sabaoths sight!" There is a pun on Sabbath and Sabaoth, "hosts," as the liberated subject, no longer a subject, contemplates the objects, no longer objects, in all their infinite variety. Spenser thus passes on to his reader the crowning act of self-identity as the contemplating of what has been made, including what one has recreated by possessing the canon of man's word as well as God's. As Wittgenstein said a generation ago, in a much misunderstood aphorism, in such an act of possession there are no more words, only the silence that marks the possession of words. A good deal has been said since then about the relation of language and silence, but real silence is the end of speech, not the stopping of it, and it is not until we have shared something of this last Sabbath vision in our greatest romance that we may begin to say that we have earned the right to silence.

NOTES

INDEX

Notes

Notes are keyed to page and line

3.19   "Apollonius story." For the Latin origin of this story, see Ben Edwin Perry, *The Ancient Romances* (1967), 300.

8.14   "George MacDonald." From an essay on Shakespeare called "St. George's Day, 1564."

8.34   "derived from myth." See A. D. Nock's critique of Karl Kerenyi in *Gnomon* (1928), 485f.

10.33   "Bede." *Ecclesiastical History*, iv, 24. The quotation is from the translation of Leo Sherley-Price, in the Penguin Classics (1955), quoted by permission of Penguin Books.

17.11   "Greek critics." See Moses Hadas, *Hellenistic Culture* (1959), 121.

20.19   "Alcuin." See H. M. Chadwick, *The Heroic Age* (1912), 41.

23.27   "Arthur Waley." See his preface to the translation of the *Ch'in Ping Mei* in Capricorn Books, 1960.

29.1   "burden of the past." See W. Jackson Bate, *The Burden of the Past and the English Poet* (1970).

35.21   "Wallace Stevens." See particularly the first essay, "The Noble Rider and the Sound of Words," in *The Necessary Angel* (1951).

37.20   "Coleridge." *Biographia Literaria*, ch. xiii.

40.16   "Scott later called him." In a letter to J. B. S. Morritt, July 24, 1814: quoted from Lockhart's *Life of Sir Walter Scott*, ch. 27.

66.32   "Saga of Harold Hardradi." See *King Harald's Saga*, tr. Magnus Magnusson and Hermann Pálsson, Penguin Classics (1966), 129, quoted by permission of Penguin Books.

68.30   "Athene." *Odyssey*, xiii, 291-299. There are many translations, but I find A. T. Murray's Loeb Library version irresistible for this passage.

70.16   "Samuel Butler." See *The Authoress of the Odyssey* (1897).

71.35   "romances." The most convenient and reliable translation of *Daphnis and Chloe* and (see below) of the *Ephesiaca* by Xenophon of Ephesus are those by Moses Hadas in *Three Greek Romances* (1953).

73.14   The quotation from Heliodorus is from Thomas Underdowne's Elizabethan translation (made not directly from the Greek but from a Latin version).

76.22   "Edmund or nobody." Except that Jane Austen, who never oversimplifies, adds a sentence remarking that Fanny's resistance might have been broken down with some increase of pressure.

86.25   "*Arcadia.*" Book I, ch. xiii (1590 version).

98.21   "Milton's phrase." *Paradise Lost*, x, 661.

100.13   "*At the Back of the North Wind.*" Cf. the reference to "Durante" in ch. x.

101.25   "myrrh." Cf. Mark 15:23; John 19:39.

108.27   "Blake." *Jerusalem*, plate 43 in some copies and editions; 29 in others.

108.33   "Chinese novel." See *The Story of the Stone*, Vol. I, tr. David Hawkes, Penguin Classics (1973), 44.

111.15   "Harlequin." See Allardyce Nicoll, *The World of Harlequin* (1963).

112.14   "Plato's phrase." *Timaeus* 35.

115.29   "The dog." See Robert Graves, *The White Goddess* (1948), 48.

116.18   "noon." Not the modern noon, but nones, the ninth hour, the time of the death of Christ on the cross.

121.23   "Jessie Weston." *From Ritual to Romance* (1920), ch. vi.

130.23   "Plutarch." *De Genio Socratis*, 21: as with Jesus' three days in the lower world, the actual interval is two nights and one day. The statement in the text comes partly from Pausanias, ix, 39.

132.29   "*Much Ado.*" Act V, sc. i, 227-228; cf. Matt. xi, 25.

137.15   "some Freudians." See Ernest Jones, *On the Nightmare* (1951).

141.8   "Students of folktale." See Margaret Schlauch, *Chaucer's Constance and Accused Queens* (1927).

143.29   "alluded to by Shakespeare." *Twelfth Night*, V, i, 116-117.

146.28 *"Handley Cross."* Ch. xlvii; the phrase "thief o' the world" is from ch. xxvi.

150.17 "Marvell's term." "The Garden," 47.

155.18 "Pygmalion." See *The Romaunt of the Rose,* tr. Harry W. Robbins (1962), 441f.

156.22 "Hymn of the Soul." I have used the translation by M. R. James, in *The Apocryphal New Testament* (1924), 411f.

162.15 "Middleton Murry." See *Keats and Shakespeare* (1925), ch. xiii.

163.1 "Anatole France." I am referring, with appropriate inaccuracy, to *L'Île des Pingouins,* III, vi. Except for the first clause in the next sentence, this passage was written before the appearance of Harold Bloom, *A Map of Misreading.*

165.12 "Gorky." See *Untimely Thoughts,* tr. Herman Ermolaev (1968), 32f.

171.32 "Wallace Stevens." *The Necessary Angel,* 142.

172.33 "Juan." See Robert Graves's poem "To Juan at the Winter Solstice."

173.34 "originally ended." *Odyssey* xxiii, 296.

175.15 "Blake." From his annotations to Wordsworth's *Poems,* 1815. For Hobbes see Spingarn, *Critical Essays of the Seventeenth Century,* Vol. I (1908), xxviii.

184.34 "Goethe." For the symbolic and poetic relevance of this in Goethe, see Peter Salm, *The Poem as Plant* (1971), 27.

185.31 "insomnia." *Finnegans Wake,* ch. v, 120.

187.19 "Hopkins." Letter to Robert Bridges, Sept. 25, 1888.

188.21 "Wittgenstein." *Tractatus Logico-Philosophicus* (1922), 7.

Index